The Case for
Servant Leadership

By Kent M. Keith

Published by Terrace Press
Printed in the United States of America.

Book and cover design by Joe Hunt
Second Edition

THE CASE FOR

SERVANT LEADERSHIP

BY KENT M. KEITH

SECOND EDITION

To the memory of
Robert K. Greenleaf
(1904-1990)
whose essay on
"The Servant as Leader"
changed my life
and the lives of millions of others

Contents

Preface to the Second Edition

I am grateful to all those who provided positive feedback regarding the first edition of *The Case for Servant Leadership*. During the past four years it has been used by a wide range of individuals as well as businesses, government agencies, non-profit organizations, hospitals, schools, and more than forty universities.

The Case for Servant Leadership was written as a short introduction or orientation to servant leadership that could also serve as a resource or springboard for those who wish to explore further. In this new edition, I have added several quotations and a few more examples of servant-leaders. I have updated the text with paragraphs summarizing scholarly definitions of servant leadership and recent research on the impacts of servant leadership in the workplace. In response to inquiries, I have created an appendix on servant leadership compared with other ideas or theories of leadership. Finally, I have added a list of sources. It is my hope that these changes will enhance the usefulness of the book for those who wish to read more.

It is also my hope that if you wish to know more about servant leadership, you will contact the Greenleaf Center for Servant Leadership (www.greenleaf.org). The Center provides publications, conferences, seminars, distance learning courses, and intensive training workshops. I encourage you to become a member of the Center, make use of its resources, meet others on the servant leadership journey, and support the worldwide servant leadership movement.

K.M.K.
June 2012

Preface to First Edition

This book is about creating a better world. There does not have to be so much pain and suffering, so much war and violence, so much starvation and disease, so many crushed dreams and untapped talents, so many problems unsolved and so many opportunities ignored. *The world does not have to be like this.*

One reason the world is like this is that people are using the power model of leadership. The purpose of this book is to make the case for the service model of leadership. It is the most ethical, relevant, practical, and effective model of leadership that I know. It is also the model of leadership that is the healthiest and most meaningful for those who lead.

Those who live the service model are called servant-leaders. This book is not an impartial assessment of servant leadership, nor a survey of the literature on servant leadership. It is about the why and how of servant leadership. It is the case for servant leadership argued by an advocate. During the past thirty years, I have served in managerial and leadership roles in the public sector, the private sector, the academic sector, and the non-profit sector. I have seen the pain and destruction that result from the power model of leadership, and I have been inspired by the humanity and effectiveness of the service model. I have no doubt that the world will be a better place when more leaders and organizations practice servant leadership.

I also have no doubt that servant leadership is best for the leader. It is the most meaningful, satisfying way to lead. It is not about self-denial or self-sacrifice. It is about *self-fulfillment.* Servant-leaders find a kind of deep happiness that is not available to other kinds of leaders.

While I am convinced that servant leadership is the best form of leadership, each person must decide for himself or herself. Such a decision often comes after a great deal of thought and experience. I have provided questions at the end of the book to stimulate individual reflection and group discussion. My hope is that each reader will not only decide to become a servant-leader, but will decide to take action—now!

K.M.K.
January 2008

1.

It Starts with the Desire to Serve

The modern servant leadership movement in America was launched by Robert K. Greenleaf. In 1970 he published his essay, *The Servant as Leader,* in which he coined the phrase "servant leadership." Greenleaf said that servant leadership begins with "the natural feeling that one wants to serve."[1]

I believe that most of us do, in fact, want to serve. When we look deeply into ourselves, most of us discover that we truly care about people, and want to make a positive difference in their lives. This "better nature" may take time to emerge, and even when it does, it can be crowded out by the pressures of daily life. But it is there. We can still hear the call of service, and we can respond.

In his book, *The Call of Service*, Robert Coles described his interviews with people who answered that "call within." One of them was Dion Diamond, a young black college student in the early 1960s who went to Louisiana to work on voter registration and stayed to fight segregation. When Coles asked him why he risked his life to do this work, Dion said: "The satisfaction, man." Coles continued:

> When I asked him about those 'satisfactions,' he said, 'I'm meeting some really fine people. I'm listening to them tell me a lot about their lives. I'm hearing them stop and think about what they're willing to do to change this world here in Louisiana. Isn't that enough—isn't that a good reason to feel satisfied? If you can spend some of your life doing work like this, then you're lucky! There may be a sheriff out there waiting for me with a gun, but if he gets me, I'll die thinking: Dion, you actually *did* something—you were part of something much bigger than yourself, and you saw people beginning to change, right before your eyes, and that was a real achievement, and that's what I mean by 'satisfaction.'[2]

The Universal Importance of Service

The satisfaction that comes from service has been recognized throughout the world. Serving others is a fundamental, universal human value. It is emphasized in the teachings of the world's great religions, as well as statements by many respected thinkers and leaders.

Jesus said that he did not come to be served, but to serve. Paul, in his letter to the Galatians, told them to carry each other's burdens. In his first letter to the Corinthians, Paul said that nobody should seek his own good, but the good of others. St. Vincent de Paul said that the highest form of worship is service to humanity. John Wesley said: "Do all the good you can, by all the means you can, in all the ways you can, in all the places you can, at all the times you can, to all the people you can, as long as ever you can." Mother Teresa said: "There is joy in transcending self to serve others."

The Jewish Talmud says: "All men are responsible for one another." An Islamic text from the Hadith of Bukhari states that "the best of men are those who are useful to others." The Sufi Sheikh, M. R. Bawa Muhaiyaddeen, said: "To realize the pain and suffering of others and to offer your hands in assistance, helping to alleviate their suffering, is Islam."

The classic Taoist text, the *Tao Te Ching*, says that "the Way of Heaven is to benefit others and not to injure." The famous Hindu text, the *Bhagavad Gita*, states: "At the beginning, mankind and the obligation of selfless service were created together. 'Through selfless service, you will always be fruitful and find the fulfillment of your desires': this is the promise of the Creator ... He is present in every act of service."[3]

The Buddhist text, the *Shantideva* or Guide to the Bodhisattva's Way of Life, says: "If I employ others for my own purposes, I myself shall experience servitude. But if I use myself for the sake of others, I shall experience only lordliness."[4]

Among great thinkers, we can quote Aristotle, who said: "What is the essence of life? To serve others and do good." Cicero, the great Roman orator and philosopher, said: "Men were brought into existence for the sake of men that they might do one another good."

Albert Schweitzer said: "The purpose of human life is to serve and to show compassion and the will to help others." Martin Luther King, Jr. said: "Life's most persistent and urgent question is: What are you doing for others?" Rabindranath Tagore, the Nobel-Prize winning Indian poet, said: "I slept and dreamed that life was joy. I awoke and saw that life was service. I acted and behold, service was joy."

There is no question that for thousands of years, serving others has been highly valued by the world's great religions and many great thinkers.

Serving the Least Privileged

Robert Greenleaf was concerned about the effect that leadership has on the least privileged in society. Throughout the centuries, in diverse cultures around the world, special emphasis has been placed on serving those in greatest need. In the appendix of his book, *The Abolition of Man,* C. S. Lewis listed statements regarding moral practices that he called "The Tao or Natural Law." Here are some examples:

> Children, old men, the poor, and the sick, should be considered as lords of the atmosphere. (Hindu)

> In the Dalebura tribe a woman, a cripple from birth, was carried about by the tribes-people in turn until her death at the age of sixty-six... They never desert the sick. (Australian Aborigine)

> I tended the old man, I gave him my staff. (Ancient Egyptian)

> You will see them take care of widows, orphans, and old men, never reproaching them. (American Indian)

> Whoso makes intercession for the weak, well pleasing is this to Samas. (Babylonian)

> I have given bread to the hungry, water to the thirsty, clothes to the naked, a ferry boat to the boatless. (Ancient Egyptian)[5]

Jesus taught his followers to help "the least of these brothers of mine." In the parable of the sheep and the goats, found in Matthew 25, he urged his followers to feed the hungry, give drink to the thirsty, provide hospitality to strangers, clothe the naked, look after the sick, and visit those in prison.

Loving and helping others gives people a profound sense of meaning and purpose that can lead to deep happiness. One reason is that it is moral. In *The Call of Service*, Robert Coles said that "all service is directly or indirectly ethical activity, a reply to a moral call within, one that answers a moral need in the world."[6]

Several years ago, my wife and our three children and I spent Christmas vacation in Cambodia. Cambodia is one of the poorest countries in the world. From 1975 to 1979, when the Khmer Rouge were in power, an estimated two million Cambodians died. Many were tortured and killed for political reasons, but most died as a result of starvation, disease, and exhaustion from forced labor.

We were in Cambodia to visit Future Light Orphanage (FLO). Phaly Nuon, the founder and Executive Director of FLO, lived through the "killing fields." She was separated from her husband, and was forced to watch as her twelve-year-old daughter was raped by Khmer Rouge soldiers. Phaly fled into the jungle to hide with her three-year-old son and her newborn baby. As the months went by, she was unable to find food, and her baby died in her arms. She survived with her son, and began to work with other women who had lost their families. She and her husband founded a refugee camp to provide counseling for those suffering post traumatic distress. In 1993, they set up FLO as a non-governmental orphanage. It is located on her family's farm land on the outskirts of Phnom Penh. Phaly also founded the FLO-Khmer Silk Processing Association, a non-profit organization that produces silk products to provide jobs for widows and generate income for FLO.

FLO is more than an orphanage—it is a safe haven for children in a society that presses them toward begging, child labor, prostitution, and drugs. Many of the children who live at FLO have lost both parents, while some have a parent who is too poor to take care of them. FLO provides food, shelter, and clothing, including school uniforms and access to public education (which is not free). In addition, FLO teaches skills that can lead to good jobs. Tourism, technology, and textiles are promising industries, so children at FLO are taught English, traditional Cambodian dance, silk and wool weaving, and how to use computers.

Phaly began with the desire to serve, and emerged as a servant-leader who is having a profound impact on the lives of thousands of children. When I asked her how she became a leader, she seemed puzzled by the question. "Because the children needed help," she said simply.

Servant-leaders have a way of attracting other servant-leaders. We learned about Phaly and FLO from Rob Hail, a retired entrepreneur and full-time servant-leader. In the fall of 2000 Rob traveled through Vietnam, Thailand, and Cambodia visiting orphanages. He was impressed by the energy and vision of Phaly at FLO. He began lining up "e-mail foster parents" for individual children. Each foster parent agrees to donate money to support a child, and commits to sending and receiving e-mail messages with the foster child every month or two. Rob quickly lined up 75 foster parents, including my wife and me.

We fell in love with the children at FLO. We talked to them, and played with them, and on Christmas day, we dressed up as Santa and his helpers and handed out presents to each of them—all 240. On our last night at the orphanage, the children performed five traditional Cambodian dances for us, fully costumed, sharing their pride and considerable skill. There was such joy in their faces as they danced! We took pictures together, and dozens of the children brought us little gifts and notes they wanted us to take back to their foster parents. There were tears then, and again at the airport the next morning. We arrived with small material gifts, and departed with large spiritual ones. Serving others is like that.

Servant leadership starts with the desire to serve—a natural, moral desire that is recognized as important by the world's great religions and many great thinkers. Service makes a difference in the lives of both those who serve and those who are served. It builds relationships that offer meaning and hope.

2.

Who Is a Servant-Leader?

The idea of the leader as facilitator or servant is not new. In fact, it can be traced back thousands of years. For example, it can be found in the teachings of Lao-Tzu and Jesus.

Early Texts

One of the earliest recorded references to the leader as a facilitator instead of an autocratic ruler comes from a passage about leaders in the *Tao Te Ching*, attributed to Lao-Tzu, a sage who lived in China sometime between 570 B.C. and 490 B.C. Here is a translation of that passage by John C. H. Wu:

> The highest type of ruler is one of whose existence
>   the people are barely aware.
> Next comes one whom they love and praise.
> Next comes one whom they fear.
> Next comes one whom they despise and defy.
>
> When you are lacking in faith,
> Others will be unfaithful to you.
>
> The Sage is self-effacing and scanty of words.
> When his task is accomplished and things have been completed,
>   All the people say, 'We ourselves have achieved it!'[7]

An interpolation by Peter Merel concludes the same passage this way:

> When the best rulers achieve their purpose
> Their subjects claim the achievement as their own.

The best leaders are almost invisible. That is why, when great deeds are done, the people have a sense of ownership and accomplishment.

In his book *The Tao of Leadership: Lao Tzu's* Tao Te Ching *Adapted for a New Age,* John Heider explained the passage on leadership this way:

17. Being a Midwife

The wise leader does not intervene unnecessarily. The leader's presence is felt, but often the group runs itself. Lesser leaders do a lot, say a lot, have followers, and form cults. Even worse ones use fear to energize the group and force to overcome resistance ....

Remember that you are facilitating another person's process. It is not your process. Do not intrude. Do not control. Do not force your own needs and insights into the foreground. If you do not trust a person's process, that person will not trust you.

Imagine that you are a midwife; you are assisting at someone else's birth. Do good without show or fuss. Facilitate what is happening rather than what you think ought to be happening. If you must take the lead, lead so that the mother is helped, yet still free and in charge. When the baby is born, the mother will rightly say: 'We did it ourselves!'[8]

Early texts encouraged leaders to care for their followers. For example, in chapter 34 of the Old Testament book of Ezekiel, the Lord tells the prophet to say: "Woe to the shepherds of Israel who only take care of themselves! Should not shepherds take care of the flock?" This was echoed more than twelve hundred years later in an Islamic *hadith* in which Mohammed said to Muslim leaders: "Verily, each of you is a shepherd, and each of you is responsible for the well being of the flock."[9]

The earliest recorded statement specifically about servant leadership was made by Jesus, who contrasted servant leadership with power-oriented leadership. He gathered his disciples together and said to them:

"You know that the rulers of the Gentiles lord it over them, and their high officials exercise authority over them. Not so with you. Instead, whoever wants to become great among you must be your servant, and whoever wants to be first must be your slave—just as the Son of Man did not come to be served, but to serve, and to give his life as a ransom for many."[10]

On his last night with his disciples, Jesus got up from the table at which they had been eating, poured water into a basin, and washed the feet of his disciples. He told them that he did this to demonstrate how they were to serve each other.[11]

Defining the Servant-Leader

In Robert Greenleaf's seminal essay on *The Servant as Leader,* he defined the servant-leader this way:

> The servant-leader *is* servant first… It begins with the natural feeling that one wants to serve, to serve *first.* Then conscious choice brings one to aspire to lead. That person is sharply different from one who is *leader* first, perhaps because of the need to assuage an unusual power drive or to acquire material possessions .... The leader-first and the servant-first are two extreme types. Between them there are shadings and blends that are part of the infinite variety of human nature.

> The difference manifests itself in the care taken by the servant-first to make sure that other people's highest priority needs are being served. The best test, and difficult to administer, is: Do those served grow as persons? Do they, *while being served,* become healthier, wiser, freer, more autonomous, more likely themselves to become servants? *And,* what is the effect on the least privileged in society? Will they benefit or at least not be further deprived?[12]

In his second major essay, *The Institution as Servant,* Greenleaf shared his credo:

> This is my thesis: caring for persons, the more able and the less able serving each other, is the rock upon which a good society is built. Whereas, until recently, caring was largely person to person, now most of it is mediated through institutions—often large, complex, powerful, impersonal; not always competent; sometimes corrupt. If a better society is to be built, one that is more just and more loving, one that provides greater creative opportunity for its people, then the most open course is to *raise both the capacity to serve and the very performance as servant of*

existing major institutions by new regenerative forces operating within them.[13]

For Greenleaf, the goal was to make the world a better place. He called upon servant-leaders to transform their organizations into servant-institutions that will impact the world in positive ways.

So who, exactly, is a servant-leader? A servant-leader is simply *a leader who is focused on serving others.* A servant-leader loves people and wants to help them. The mission of the servant-leader is therefore to identify and meet the needs of others. Loving and helping others gives a servant-leader meaning and satisfaction in life.

Servant-leaders can be government officials, business executives, academic administrators, non-profit leaders, military commanders, coaches, friends, or neighbors. Servant-leaders do most of the things that other leaders do—they articulate a vision, they manage, they communicate, and so forth. What sets servant-leaders apart from other leaders is their desire to serve. As a result, they are focused on others, not just themselves, and they are motivated to make life better for others, not just for themselves. This difference in focus and motivation is what really distinguishes servant-leaders, regardless of their titles, roles, or positions.

What are the characteristics of a servant-leader? In his essay *The Servant as Leader,* Greenleaf made it clear that the most important characteristic was the desire to serve. He also emphasized listening and understanding; acceptance and empathy; foresight; awareness; persuasion; conceptualization; self-healing; and rebuilding community. He said that servant-leaders initiate action, are goal-oriented, are dreamers of great dreams, are good communicators, are able to withdraw and re-orient themselves, and are dependable, trusted, creative, intuitive, and situational.

Larry Spears identified ten characteristics of the servant-leader: listening, empathy, healing, awareness, persuasion, conceptualization, foresight, stewardship, commitment to the growth of people, and building community.[14]

Bill Turner, former Chairman and CEO of W.C. Bradley Company and Synovus Financial, developed his own list of the common qualities of servant-leaders. Those qualities are unconditional love, brokenness, self-awareness, being real, foresight, facilitating a common vision, building community, empowering others, meeting the needs of others and removing obstacles, and being a cheerleader.[15]

The Center for Servant Leadership at the Pastoral Institute in Columbus, Georgia, describes servant leadership as a lifelong journey that includes discovery of one's self, a desire to serve others, and a commitment to lead. The servant-leader is someone who continuously strives to be trustworthy, self-aware, humble, caring, visionary, empowering, relational, competent, a good steward, and a community builder.

Scholars are identifying characteristics of servant leadership in order to develop and test theories about the impact of servant leadership. For example, Robert C. Liden and his colleagues identified nine dimensions of servant leadership that they used in their research: emotional healing, creating value for the community, conceptual skills, empowering, helping subordinates grow and succeed, putting subordinates first, behaving ethically, relationships, and servanthood.[16] Dirk van Dierendonck reviewed the scholarly literature and identified six key characteristics of servant-leader behavior: empowering and developing people, humility, authenticity, interpersonal acceptance, providing direction, and stewardship.[17]

Whatever their qualities or characteristics, servant-leaders have a desire to serve. Some start out that way, early in life. Others start out with a desire for power, wealth, and fame, and then discover that there is more joy in serving others. Leadership becomes meaningful when it is a way of helping others.

Examples of Servant-Leaders in History

There are no doubt thousands of examples of servant-leaders in history, literature, the movies, and daily life today. One thinks of historical figures like George Washington, Abraham Lincoln, Florence Nightingale, Susan B. Anthony, Albert Schweitzer, Gandhi, Martin Luther King, Jr., Nelson Mandela, Cesar Chavez, and Mother Teresa. Three of my favorites are

George Williams, Harriet Tubman, and Eiichi Shibusawa.

George Williams was a young man who worked in a draper's shop in London in 1844. He was a sales assistant, and like lots of other young men in London at the time, he worked ten to twelve hours a day, six days a week. At night, he slept in a crowded room over his workplace. Williams noticed that young men like himself had few positive alternatives to life on the streets. So he gathered together a group of other drapers, and they formed a Christian fellowship of young men who were committed to helping each other grow in mind and spirit. That group became the YMCA, which today serves forty-five million men, women, and children through hundreds of programs in 124 countries.

Harriet Tubman was born into slavery in 1822. As a teenage field hand, she was nearly killed when hit in the head by an iron weight thrown by an overseer at a fleeing slave. That injury plagued her for the rest of her life. When her owner died in 1849, she traveled the Underground Railroad to freedom in Philadelphia. The Underground Railroad was a secret series of houses, tunnels, and roads set up by abolitionists and former slaves to provide an escape route for slaves. From 1850 to 1860, Tubman traveled to the South about eighteen times, and helped three hundred slaves escape to freedom, including her brothers and parents. She settled many of them in Canada, where they could not be recaptured. Southerners tried to put a stop to her work by putting out rewards for her capture. She was reverently called "Moses" by the slaves she helped to freedom.

During the Civil War, Tubman provided nursing care for black soldiers and newly freed slaves in Union camps. She spied and scouted behind Confederate lines, and even led a military raid on a Confederate outpost, freeing 700 slaves. After the war, she became a community activist and campaigned for women's rights. Toward the end of her life, she established a home for the aged on land next to her own house in Auburn, New York. Tubman was a servant-leader, fighting for the freedom and rights of others.

Eiichi Shibusawa was a Japanese industrialist who lived from 1840 to 1931. Shibusawa was born into the peasant class. At the age of twenty-seven he visited Europe, and came to understand the importance of industrial and economic development. When the Meiji Restoration began, he became a member of the elite Ministry of Finance. He left the ministry to become president of Japan's first modern bank. Using the bank as his base, he began building the economy of Japan by establishing businesses of all kinds. During his lifetime he founded and developed more than six hundred industrial companies, creating tens of thousands of jobs.

Shibusawa's focus was on maximizing talent—developing human capital. He believed that good ethics and business should go together. He served as an unofficial management counselor, helping hundreds of civil servants, businessmen, and managers. He also organized training programs, supported higher education for women, and engaged in projects to promote social welfare. One of his legacies was the establishment of a famous university of economics. Shibusawa was a servant-leader, focused on building his nation by creating opportunities for his fellow countrymen.

Servant-Leaders in Our Communities

While there have been many famous servant-leaders, most servant-leaders have not been known outside the group or community they have served. They did not seek fame, they sought to make a difference—and they did.

Servant-leaders are active throughout the world in the Rotary movement, where "Service Above Self" has long been a cherished motto. Founded in 1905, Rotary has approximately 1.2 million members working in 34,000 clubs in more than two hundred countries and geographical areas. Rotary International launched a polio eradication program in 1988, when polio was common throughout the world. Since then, Rotarians and their partner agencies have immunized more than two billion children in 122 countries, reducing polio from 350,000 cases in 1988 to fewer than 650 cases in 2011—a 99.8 percent reduction. It is estimated that four million children who might have contracted polio have been saved from the crippling disease. Rotarians raised more than $1 billion, and tens of thousands of Rotarians have assisted in distributing the polio vaccine.

Individuals make a difference. For example, Will Hartzell is a friend of mine who learned that each year contaminated drinking water causes the deaths of millions of people around the world. He made a deep personal commitment to change that. He developed solar water pasteurizers that are a simple, low-cost, long-term solution to the problem. In spite of all the "naysayers" who told him it couldn't be done, he launched his company, Safe Water Systems, in 1996. Will recalled:

> One safe-drinking-water project that left an indelible impact on me was in Africa. Our Solar Water Pasteurizers were installed in five locations near Arusha, Tanzania. One site was the Selian Hospital. The hospital was not able to afford a water disinfection system and ran the risk of patients actually contracting diseases while at the hospital.
>
> After our equipment was installed, I was watching the patients as they came to get clean water to drink. One woman was in the hospital because her child was gravely ill. After she filled her water bottle and was headed back to her child, she stopped and looked at me. Our eyes met in one of those time-stopping moments. We didn't speak the same language, but the nurse translated for me. She said, "Thank you. Thank you for giving my child the chance to live."
>
> At that moment I knew that I would do whatever it took to provide safe drinking water for as many people as I could all over the world.[18]

Since then, Will and his colleagues have installed 4,000 solar water pasteurizers and other water purification systems in fifty-three countries. The result is that 400,000 people in those countries no longer risk illness or death because of contaminated water. Will Hartzell is a servant-leader who saves lives every day.

After the racial riots in Detroit in 1967, Eleanor Josaitis and her friend and pastor Father William Cunningham decided to do something. Father Cunningham left his teaching job at a seminary and began working at a parish in the inner city. Eleanor and her husband sold their suburban home and moved their family to a neighborhood where rioting had occurred. Together, Josaitis and Cunningham founded an organization they called Focus: HOPE that is dedicated to providing practical solutions to racism and poverty.

During the next thirty years, they built an organization that provides food for women and children; fights discriminatory grocery prices in low-income neighborhoods; operates a Montessori preschool for students and community members; creates employment opportunities through a Machinist Training Institute; runs a FAST TRACK program to help students improve their reading and math skills so they can enter training programs; and offers a First Step program in reading and math to help students qualify for FAST TRACK.

By 2007, Focus: HOPE had trained more than 2,700 qualified machinists and graduated nearly 6,000 people from First Step and FAST TRACK. Their Center for Advanced Technologies graduated more than one hundred manufacturing engineers with associate or bachelor degrees granted by cooperating universities, and their Information Technology Center had graduated nearly six hundred students. And Focus: HOPE was feeding 43,000 low-income elderly, mothers, and children each month.[19] Cunningham and Josaitis demonstrated how servant-leaders can transform neighborhoods and create opportunities that change the lives of thousands of people.

Takeshi Oishi was an educator, serving forty years as a teacher and principal of an elementary school in Japan. Toward the end of his career, he became a member of a government committee that studied social issues. During that time, he learned about the plight of the mentally challenged and their need for specially designed housing and training.

When Mr. Oishi retired, he looked for land that could be used to build a home for mentally challenged individuals. He not only found an appropriate site—he convinced the owner to donate the land. It took years to negotiate the permits and approvals, raise the money, and complete construction, but the new center was finally built. When Mr. Oishi died in 1995, all fifty of the residents of the center attended his funeral, sitting in the front row to pay their respects to the man who had given them a home. Takeshi Oishi was a servant-leader who identified and met the special needs of others.

Servant-Leaders in Fiction

Robert Greenleaf's concept of the servant-leader was stimulated by his reading of *Journey to the East* by Herman Hesse. It is the story of a group of travelers who were served by Leo, who did their menial chores and lifted them with his spirit and his song. All went well until Leo disappeared one day. The travelers fell into disarray and could go no farther on their own. The journey was over. Years later, one of the travelers saw Leo again—as the revered head of the Order that sponsored the journey. Leo, who was their servant, was the titular head of the Order, a great and noble leader. Greenleaf observed that "this story clearly says that *the great leader is seen as servant first,* and that simple fact is the key to his greatness. Leo was actually the leader all of the time, but he was servant first because that was what he was, *deep down inside.*"[20]

One of my favorite servant-leaders in fiction is Atticus Finch, the father and attorney in *To Kill a Mockingbird,* the Pulitzer-Prize winning novel by Harper Lee. The story is set in a small southern town during the depression of the 1930s. Atticus Finch, portrayed in the movie by Gregory Peck, is a lawyer who defended a black man, Tom Robinson, who was unjustly accused of raping a white girl. In a time of racial passions, the jury ignored the obvious facts. Atticus lost the trial, and Tom, who was certain that there was no hope in appealing his conviction, was shot when he tried to escape.

Although Atticus lost the trial, what was important is that he placed himself in service to another, and at great personal risk, stood for what was right. Those around him respected his quiet courage. Immediately after the jury issued its guilty verdict, Atticus said some reassuring words to Tom, chatted briefly with the court reporter, and then began packing up his books and papers. Members of the black community, who were sitting in the balcony, watched him packing up. One by one, they stood up, in a silent gesture of respect. His daughter was in the balcony with them, and as Atticus turned to leave the courtroom, Reverend Sykes leaned over and said to her: "Miss Jean Louise! Miss Jean Louise! Stand up. Your father's passing!"

In fantasy novels, there are wizards who are servant-leaders, such as Gandalf in *The Lord of the Rings* by J. R. R. Tolkien, Belgarath in *The Belgariad* by David Eddings, and Ged in *The Earthsea Trilogy* by Ursula Le Guin. Each wizard provides wisdom and guidance, and makes sacrifices for the good of the group.

Another great example of a servant-leader is Hazel-rah, the Chief

Rabbit in the novel *Watership Down* by Richard Adams. This is a wonderful fable about a group of rabbits who set out to find a new home. Hazel-rah becomes the Chief Rabbit, not because he is the biggest rabbit in the group, or the most clever, or the most clairvoyant. He becomes the leader because he is willing to listen, and he often asks for advice from others. He knows the different strengths of the other rabbits, and draws out those strengths for the good of the group. He is able to identify the needs of the group, and make decisions and take action in a way that unites the rabbits in seeking to achieve their common goals. And he is willing to pitch in and take personal risks on behalf of the group. The rabbits face hard times, and are severely tested, but with Hazel-rah's guidance, they work together as a team, and they succeed in finding a new home.

One of the many movies made by Kurosawa Akira is titled *Ikiru*, which means "to live" in Japanese. It is the story of Kanji Watanabe, a Japanese government bureaucrat who discovered that he was dying of cancer and had only six months to live. After wandering around the city feeling sorry for himself, he decided to make a difference before he died.

Watanabe set out to establish a playground for a neighborhood whose children had no place to play. The mothers of the neighborhood had approached the government and asked that a playground be built, but they had been referred from government agency to government agency, each bureaucrat passing the buck to the other. Nobody was willing to take responsibility and help them. Watanabe, a branch chief in the Citizen's Section, decided to take up their cause. While enduring great physical pain, he patiently and courageously confronted each obstacle until he got the playground built. He died late one night, sitting in one of the swings in the playground, softly singing one of his favorite songs, completely at peace with himself. At last his life meant something. He had helped somebody. He had become a servant-leader, and he had made a difference.

3.

Power Model vs. Service Model

In his definition of the servant-leader, Greenleaf distinguished between the servant-first and the leader-first. The servant-first lives the *service* model of leadership. The leader-first lives the *power* model of leadership.[21] The power model is *neither* moral nor effective, while the service model is *both* moral and effective.

According to the power model, leadership is about how to accumulate and wield power, how to make people do things, how to attack and win. It is about clever strategies, applying pressure, and manipulating people to get what you want. A word that is often used is *realpolitik*. It means politics and the exercise of power with no reference to morality or ethics.

Problems with the Power Model

There are some severe problems with the power model. First, the power model focuses on *having* power, not on using it wisely. Power is an end in itself. This leads to the second problem, which is that the power model defines success or victory in terms of *who gains more power*, not in terms of who accomplishes the most for his or her organization or community. Factions may brilliantly battle other factions, and great victories and defeats may occur between them, with no benefit to the organization or society at large. In fact, rather than healing and building, factional warfare between rival power groups usually results in more hurt and more fragmentation.

A third problem with the power model of leadership is that it promotes conflict between power groups. A person wants to be a leader, and since he has been told that leadership is about power, he builds his power base. But then, other would-be leaders are building their power bases, too. Pretty soon, leaders in the power model are so focused on fighting rival power factions, that they have little time to focus on problems that need to be solved or opportunities that need to be seized. And without that focus, organizations and communities don't move forward. The problems continue, and the dreams go unfulfilled.

Other problems with the power model relate to the leader herself or himself. People who seek power often become irrelevant as leaders. They focus on what *they* want, instead of what other people want, and they lose touch with the people they are supposed to be serving. Of course, they may remain in power because they are good at maintaining their power base, but even then, they may never be happy. That's because people who seek power can never get enough of it. Power becomes a kind of addiction or disease. They always want more, and more, and more. This easily results in spiritual corruption and an unhappy life of self-torment.

An example from literature is Shakespeare's *Macbeth*, a tragedy set in medieval Scotland. Macbeth is a loyal and courageous Scottish general who defeats an invading army. He encounters a group of witches who prophesy that he will be thane of Cawdor and eventually king, while the heirs of another Scottish general, Banquo, will also become kings in their day.

Then Macbeth learns that as a reward for his victory, King Duncan has just made him the thane of Cawdor. With the first part of the prophesy fulfilled, Macbeth's ambition becomes so strong that he abandons all moral constraints. Encouraged by his wife, he murders King Duncan, and then, as a cover-up, blames and murders two chamberlains. He also hires murderers to kill Banquo, and after receiving further prophesies from the witches, he orders the murders of the wife and children of Macduff, a Scottish nobleman who opposes him. Macbeth becomes a tyrant, feared by all. Lady Macbeth, haunted by all the bloodshed, goes insane and finally commits suicide. Duncan's son raises an army in England, and with the support of other Scottish nobles, the army defeats Macbeth, who is killed by Macduff in combat.

The central theme is that Macbeth wanted power, and his ambition corrupted him. He abandoned his loyalty and morality, and became a murderer. But becoming the king wasn't enough for him. Macbeth became paranoid. He knew that there were others who could take his power from him. He didn't want to give up his power, so he continued killing. Power was addictive, and he could never be at peace.

A modern literary example was provided by Robert Penn Warren, who won a Pulitzer Prize for his brilliant novel, *All the King's Men*. The novel is about the transformation of Willie Stark from a country lawyer with good intentions to a power-hungry politician. He began by fighting the corrupt political machine. He got elected governor, and did good things for the people. But his desire for power gradually swallowed his desire to serve, and he became the head of his own corrupt political machine. It is a brooding, unsettling story of a man who set out to serve others, and ended by making them serve him.

Sometimes, people think they are serving others, but are really using the power model instead. In his essay on *The Servant as Leader*, Greenleaf mentioned Ken Kesey's book, *One Flew Over the Cuckoo's Nest*. Greenleaf noted that the nurse in the novel was strong, able, dedicated, dominating, authority-ridden, manipulative, and exploitative. The net effect of her influence "diminished other people, literally destroyed them."[22] She did battle with MacMurphy, a patient who helped others to become healthier and stronger. We feel the pain and loss when the nurse wins, and MacMurphy dies.

Machiavelli and the Amoral Use of Power

Perhaps the most famous intellectual to argue for the amoral use of raw power was Niccolo Machiavelli, who lived in Florence in the fifteenth century. According to scholar Max Lerner, Machiavell's book *The Prince* is "one of the half dozen books that have done most to shape Western thought."[23] Perhaps that is why the power model is so dominant in our culture.

Lerner said that Machiavelli rejected theology and idealism in favor of "political realism." He abandoned what was ethical in favor of what was "realistic." For example, in *The Prince*, Machiavelli argued that "in taking a state the conqueror must arrange to commit all his cruelties at once, so as not to have to recur to them every day."[24] He said that since so many people are not good, "it is necessary for a prince, who wishes to maintain himself, to learn how not to be good ..."[25] He urged that "a prudent ruler ought not to keep faith when by so doing it would be against his interest, and when the reasons which made him bind himself no longer exist."[26] Since it looks good when a leader overcomes difficulties, "a wise prince ought, when he has the chance, to foment astutely some enmity, so that by suppressing it he will augment his greatness."[27]

Most of us are fascinated by power, and many of us want to have some. We may be tempted by the "realistic" approach that advises the use of raw power, an approach that is especially easy to find in the works of military and political strategists. A recent example is Robert Greene's book, *The 48 Laws of Power*. The book jacket, which is designed to sell the book, says:

> The bestselling book for those who want POWER, watch POWER, or want to arm themselves against POWER. Amoral, cunning, ruthless, and instructive, this piercing work distills three thousand years of the history of power into forty-eight well-explicated laws ... synthesizing the philosophies of Machiavelli, Sun-tzu, Carl von Clausewitz, and other great thinkers.

Greene said in his Preface:

> The feeling of having no power over people and events is generally unbearable to us—when we feel helpless we feel miserable. No one wants less power; everyone wants more. In the world today, however, it is dangerous to seem too power hungry, to be overt with your power moves. We have to seem fair and decent. So we need to be subtle— congenial yet cunning, democratic yet devious.[28]

The so-called "laws of power" that are described in Greene's book are based on deceit, cunning, treachery, and conquest, all for personal gain. They are about hiding your intentions, grabbing the credit, keeping people dangling, being selectively honest, pretending to be a friend while being a spy, and exploiting people's need to believe. Should we wonder why the world is the way that it is, when the power model is the dominant model of leadership?

Morality is about right and wrong behavior. The power model is not really concerned with that—it is concerned with acquiring and wielding power. If pretending to care about people is good for acquiring power, the power-seeking leader will pretend to care. The leader will identify some needs, and will make promises about meeting those needs. But once in power, the leader may do little to implement those promises. In fact the leader is likely to do just enough, and *only* just enough, to keep his or her power. Even worse, a leader may make caring statements, and then do the opposite.

If a leader who lives the power model can gain power without helping anybody, he or she will do so. In fact, the leader may feel justified in making life *worse* for a lot of people, so long as he or she gains power. Power is self-justifying; power itself is the end. It is not a means to make life better for others, except the power holders and their close friends. That is why *leaders who live the power model are not very effective in meeting human needs or making life better for others. It's not what they are trying to do.* It's not their focus. It's not what they care about. Often, they can gain and maintain power while being remarkably indifferent to the needs of others.

Servant Leadership Has a Moral Base

Unlike the power model, the service model does have a moral base. The whole point of the service model is to be of service—to identify and meet the needs of others. It is about paying attention to others and treating them right.

To accept the reality of pain and suffering in the world, and only exploit it for private gain, is morally wrong and ignores all the higher aspirations of human beings since time immemorial—aspirations found in moral and ethical codes, as well as religious and spiritual teachings. These aspirations are made all the more urgent by the daily cries for help of those who are disadvantaged. The power model perpetuates fear, war, violence, disease, and starvation. If people continue to use the power model, we will make little progress in bringing peace or justice to the world.

Machiavelli and Greene say: This is the way the world is—turn it to your personal advantage. We need to hear a different voice, a voice that says: Here is the way the world *could* be—let's turn it to *everyone's* advantage.

Greenleaf said that "caring for persons, the more able and the less able serving each other, is the rock upon which a good society is built."[29] And that is what servant-leaders do, by living the service model of leadership. The servant-leader does not ask, "How can I get power? How can I make people do things?" The servant-leader asks, "What do people need? How can I help them to get it? What does my organization need to do? How can I help my organization to do it?" Thus, rather than embarking on a quest for personal power, the servant-leader embarks on a quest to identify and meet the needs of others. It is this daily quest that results in improving organizations and the lives of the people they serve; it is this daily quest that lifts communities and societies for the benefit of all.

For Servant-Leaders Power Is Only a Tool

Of course, we live in a real world. We know that power abhors a vacuum. Somebody is going to exercise power, and it makes a difference who that somebody is. Certainly, a servant-leader can accumulate and exercise power. A servant-leader can even become angry and enter the fray to do battle. What is important is that the servant-leader accumulates power or becomes angry *on behalf of others*. A servant-leader acts in response to the way *others* are treated, not in response to the way he or she is treated. The servant-leader knows that power is a means, not an end. It is only a tool. Often, it is not even the most important tool. There are many tools, such as listening and coaching, that turn out to be more important than power.

Because power is only a tool, great servant-leaders have been willing to give it up when they no longer need it to serve others. Cincinnatus, George Washington, and Jose de San Martin are good examples. They made the leadership contribution that was needed at the time, and then passed the power to others.

Cincinnatus was a Roman political leader and general who lived in the fifth century B.C. He is a semi-legendary figure often cited as a model of Roman virtue. He lived a simple life, working on his own farm. He served as a Roman consul in 460 B.C. When the Aequi tribe and the Volscians threatened Rome in 458 B.C., the Senate begged Cincinnatus to become the absolute dictator and save Rome. Cincinnatus was reluctant to become the absolute dictator, because he was needed on the farm. If his crops weren't sown in a timely manner, his family could starve. But he agreed to serve. Organizing the troops, he defeated the Aequi and Volscians in sixteen days. He then resigned his absolute authority, and returned to farming. He came out of retirement to do the same thing again, twenty years later.

George Washington is sometimes described as a modern Cincinnatus. Washington was a surveyor and a farmer, widely respected as a person of good character who was focused on public service. He was the general of the Continental Army, president of the Constitutional Convention, and the first president of the United States. He was so admired that if he had wanted to be king, the United States might have become a constitutional monarchy. But that is not what Washington wanted. He didn't want to be king, he wanted to be a public servant. He voluntarily resigned his commission as general after the war, and later, after two terms as president, he decided not to run again, giving the nation a successful transition of power. Historian Joseph Ellis said that Washington was "the supreme example of the leader who could be trusted with power because he was so ready to give it up."[30]

Jose de San Martin is another famous leader who twice gave up his power. Born in 1778 in what is now Argentina, San Martin received a military education in Spain and served in the Spanish Army. In 1812 he returned to Argentina to join the rebels who were fighting to free South America from Spanish rule. Although Argentina was declared independent in 1816, San Martin knew that Argentina would not remain independent if the Spanish still controlled Chile and Peru. In 1817 he joined Chilean leader Bernardo O'Higgins and led an army of 5,000 men on a dangerous march through the snowy Andes mountains to Chile, where they defeated the Spanish. Chile was declared independent in 1818. San Martin declined to be the Chilean president, giving that honor to O'Higgins instead.

San Martin next assembled a fleet and sailed north to attack the Spanish at Peru. In 1821 he declared Peru an independent nation, and was named the governor. When his vision of how to organize the newly independent countries of South America came in conflict with another patriot, Simon Bolivar, who had been fighting further north, San Martin deferred to Bolivar, returned to Argentina, and eventually retired in Europe. Many Argentineans consider San Martin their greatest national hero. He fought for others, not himself, and he gave up his power to others, rather than keeping it for himself.

Power as a Gift

The paradox is that a servant-leader can gain power without seeking it. People trust servant-leaders, and give them power, because they know that servant-leaders use power to benefit everyone. James Autry wrote:

> … [T]rue power comes from the people. It comes from gaining the trust and support of the people who then give you the power. Power is like love. The more you try to give it to others, the more it just seems to flow to you naturally.[31]

Power is given to a servant-leader as a gift, by others who trust the leader. So long as the servant-leader continues to serve others well, there is no reason for anyone to take back their gift of power.

On the other hand, when a leader grabs power, the leader will constantly have to fight to keep it. If the leader had to grab it, it means that others don't want the leader to have it, or they want it for themselves instead. The leader will constantly be defending his turf. After all, if the leader grabbed power, somebody else can grab it back, just because *they* want it. So the leader has to keep fighting rivals, and building ever-shifting alliances, and trying to be the power broker, and trying to defeat the plans of others so they will not get credit for accomplishing things that might in turn enhance their power and threaten the leader. The leader ends up being so busy defending his turf, that he really doesn't have time to do much else.

People Want to Follow Servant-Leaders

When servant-leaders work on problems and opportunities, they don't carry a lot of ego baggage. They don't worry about their own personal status or prestige. They just focus on the problem or opportunity. That makes it a lot easier for people to work with them and follow them. It makes it easier to build teams and partnerships and get things done. There's an old saying, "it's amazing how much we get done around here when nobody cares who gets the credit." That's what servant-leaders are like. They are focused on the work, not the credit.

Servant-leaders are human and make mistakes. However, people are willing to follow servant-leaders because they know that servant-leaders are not in it for themselves. As Greenleaf wrote in his essay, *The Servant as Leader:*

> A fresh critical look is being taken at the issues of power and authority, and people are beginning to learn, however haltingly, to relate to one another in less coercive and more creatively supporting ways. A new moral principle is emerging which holds that the only authority deserving one's allegiance is that which is freely and knowingly granted by the led to the leader in response to, and in proportion to, the clearly evident servant stature of the leader. Those who choose to follow this principle will not casually accept the authority of existing institutions. *Rather, they will freely respond only to individuals who are chosen as leaders because they are proven and trusted as servants.* To the extent that this principle prevails in the future, the only truly viable institutions will be those that are predominantly servant-led.[32]

A servant-leader is by far the best leader to take an organization through a period of change. The reason is that a servant-leader will not use organizational change as the excuse for building his or her own power and position. The servant-leader will not make changes based on personalities, factional politics, and competition between rivals. The servant-leader will be focused instead on meeting the needs of the organization and those it serves. The servant-leader will be listening, consulting, and analyzing information so that the organization can adapt and remain relevant to changing needs. Hard decisions may have to be made, but if so, they will be made by giving priority to the needs of others.

The Unifying Dream

Servant-leaders know that it is not about them, it is about making a difference. Often, they are able to unite their colleagues through the development of a shared dream or vision of a better future. In his essay, *The Leadership Crisis*, Greenleaf said:

> ... Institutions function better when the idea, the dream, is to the fore, and the person, the leader, is seen as the servant of the idea. It is not 'I,' the ultimate leader, that is moving this institution to greatness; it is the dream, the great idea. 'I' am subordinate to the idea; 'I' am servant of the idea along with everyone else who is involved in the effort .... The leader leads well when leadership is, and is seen as, serving the dream and searching for a better one .... It is the *idea* that unites people in the common effort, not the charisma of the leader. It is the communicated faith of the leader in the dream that enlists dedicated support needed to move people toward accomplishment of the dream.[33]

Servant-leaders help their colleagues to develop, articulate, and work toward a dream that is inspiring and truly meets the needs of others.

Service, Love, and Community

Greenleaf pointed out that serving each other requires love. He noted that love is undefinable. "But it begins, I believe, with one absolute condition: unlimited liability! As soon as one's liability for another is qualified to any degree, love is diminished by that much."[34] Greenleaf went on to say that "any human service where the one who is served should be loved in the process requires community, a face-to-face group in which the liability of each for the other and all for one is unlimited, or as close to it as it is possible to get."[35]

Bill Turner emphasized the importance of building a community as part of his journey in building successful companies like Synovus Financial, which *Fortune* magazine rated the #1 Best Company to Work for in America in 1999. In his book, *The Learning of Love: A Journey Toward Servant Leadership*, Turner said:

> Servant leadership must be grounded in a love that is a spiritual gift. And it must reach outside the organization in many ways to create a caring community and ultimately to build a better world. In a servant-

led organization, the basis for all decision making should be, 'What is the loving thing to do?'

There is a deep spiritual hunger in all of us to find a place where people really care for one another, where we can find something to believe in and something and someone to trust. When these things are discovered together in community, great things can happen. Believing in the worth and goodness of people is basic to servant leadership.[36]

Juana Bordas, in her book *Salsa, Soul and Spirit*, points out that "servant leadership is deeply anchored in Black, American Indian, and Latino cultures that center on community responsibility, the public welfare, and addressing the social structures that hinder people's progress."[37] These ethnic groups have defined leadership as community servanthood—serving the collective. "Leaders, therefore, are like good stewards who build community capacity and group empowerment."[38] Because the leaders understand that their first responsibility is to promote the good of the entire community, people trust their leaders and are willing to place the community in their hands.

Bordas said that "leaders grow their communities by engaging people in the following practices: (1) encouraging participation and building consensus, (2) creating a community of leaders, (3) generating a shared vision, (4) using culturally effective communication, and (5) weaving partnerships and connections."[39] The "top" leadership positions are often rotated among individuals, because leadership does not belong to a person, it belongs to the community. Leaders set high standards and follow the same rules as other community members. It is expected that leaders will not take more than their fair share of community resources. Leadership is not about the power of an individual, but rather, the good of all.

This focus on building and serving the larger community is a key difference between the power model and the service model of leadership. In her talk on "The Work of the Servant-Leader," Margaret Wheatley said:

> There are many patterns, many beliefs, out there about leadership, about people, about motivation, about human development. The essential truth I'm discovering right now is that when we are together, more becomes possible. When we are together, joy is available. In the

midst of a world that is insane, that will continue to surprise us with new outrages ... in the midst of that future, the gift is each other. We have lived with a belief system that has not told us that. We have lived with a belief that has said, 'We're in it for ourselves. It's a dog-eat-dog world out there. Only the strong survive and you can't trust anybody.' That's the belief that's operating in most organizations if you scratch the surface. The belief that called you to be a servant-leader, I believe, is the belief of who we are as a species. We have need for each other. We have a desire for each other, and, more and more, I believe that if the *real work is to stay together*, then we are not only the best resource to move into this future—we are the only resource .... We need to learn how to be together: that is the essential work of the servant-leader.[40]

Simple Ways to Contrast the Power and Service Models

There are some simple ways to contrast a power-oriented leader and a service-oriented leader. The first is this: Power-oriented leaders want to *make* people do things. Servant-leaders want to *help* people do things. That's why servant-leaders are usually facilitators, coordinators, healers, partners, and coalition-builders.

Another way to contrast the two models is this. The power model assumes a hierarchy shaped like a pyramid. Only a few people have power—those at the top of the pyramid—so it is assumed that only they can be leaders. In the service model, the hierarchy doesn't matter. That's because *anybody* in a family, organization, or community can be of service. *Anybody* can identify and meet the needs of others. *Anybody* can be a servant-leader.

At bottom, the difference between the two models is simple. The power model is about *grabbing*. The service model is about *giving*.

We have to decide. Are we going to grab, or give? Are we going to *use* people, or *help* people? It's a fundamental moral decision. Albert Einstein said: "The high destiny of the individual is to serve rather than to rule." Servant leadership is a way to work toward that high destiny.

4.

The Key Practices
of Servant-Leaders

Servant leadership is not only a moral approach to leadership, it is also the most effective way of leading. Servant leadership really *works*, and it works in all types of organizations, in all sectors—public, private, non-profit, and academic.

Robert Greenleaf worked for AT&T when it was one of the largest corporations in the world. His final role there was Director of Management Research. He continually sought ways to improve the leadership and management of the company. After retiring from AT&T, he reflected, and concluded that the best approach to leadership is servant leadership. Many experts agree.

What the Experts Say

Ken Blanchard met Robert Greenleaf in the late 1960s when Blanchard was at Ohio University and Greenleaf came to spend a weekend with the students. Blanchard is convinced that servant leadership is the foundation for effective leadership. He said:

> I truly believe that servant leadership has never been more applicable to the world of leadership than it is today. Not only are people looking for a deeper purpose and meaning when they must meet the challenges of today's changing world; they are also looking for principles and philosophies that actually work. Servant leadership works. Servant leadership is about getting people to a higher level by leading people at a higher level.[41]

In *Leading at a Higher Level*, Blanchard said: "Servant leadership is not just another management technique. It is a way of life for those with servant hearts."[42] Blanchard argued that servant leadership provides better leadership because the vision and values are established up front, and servant leadership requires the kind of humility that brings out the best in both the leaders and those they serve. Servant leadership also results in better service, because frontline people are encouraged and empowered to develop strong relationships with customers. Servant leadership creates high performing organizations, because it supports shared power and high involvement throughout the organization. Servant-leaders capitalize on diversity in cultures, styles, social relationships, race, religion, sexual orientation, and age. They know that when people—all their people—are involved in decisions that affect their lives, they are healthier, happier, feel less stress, and have a greater sense of ownership and commitment. Finally, organizations led by servant-leaders are more likely to generate both success and significance—both bottom line results and the meaning that comes from generosity, service, and loving relationships.[43]

Stephen Covey is also a champion of servant leadership. He said:

> The deepest part of human nature is that which urges people— each one of us—to rise above our present circumstances and to transcend our nature. If you can appeal to it, you tap into a whole new source of human motivation. Perhaps that is why I have found Robert Greenleaf's teaching on servant leadership to be so enormously inspiring, so uplifting, so ennobling.
>
> A great movement is taking place throughout the world today. Its roots, I believe, are to be found in two powerful forces. One is the dramatic globalization of markets and technology. And in a very pragmatic way, this tidal wave of change is fueling the impact of the second force: timeless, universal principles that have governed, and always will govern, all enduring success, especially those principles that give 'air' and 'life' and creative power to the human spirit that *produces* value in markets, organizations, families, and, most significantly, individual's lives.
>
> One of these fundamental, timeless principles is the idea of servant leadership, and I am convinced that it will continue to dramatically increase in its relevance ...[44]

Experts in business leadership and management often describe the effective leader as a servant-leader without using the words "servant-leader." For example, Peter Drucker, in his book *The Effective Executive*, said that the key question that distinguishes an executive is the question: "What can I contribute?" Drucker said:

> The effective executive focuses on contribution .... He asks: 'What can I contribute that will significantly affect the performance and the results of the institution I serve?' .... The focus on contribution turns the executive's attention away from his own specialty, his own narrow skills, his own department, and toward the performance of the whole ... to the entire organization and its purpose. He therefore will also come to think in terms of the customer, the client, or the patient, who is the ultimate reason for whatever the organization produces ...[45]

Drucker described the effective executive as someone who is focused on contribution and focused on others—a good definition of servant leadership in business.

Peter M. Senge is the author of *The Fifth Discipline* and a founder of the Society for Organizational Learning. In a talk published in *Reflections on Leadership*, he said:

> I believe that the book Servant Leadership, and in particular the essay, "The Servant as Leader," which starts the book off, is the most singular and useful statement on leadership that I have read in the last 20 years. Despite the virtual tidal wave of books on leadership during the last few years, there is something different about Bob Greenleaf's essay, something both simpler and more profound .... For many years, I simply told people not to waste their time reading all the other managerial leadership books. 'If you are really serious about the deeper territory of true leadership,' I would say, 'read Greenleaf.'[46]

While scholarly research is still at an early stage, the results so far indicate that servant leadership encourages positive organizational citizenship behaviors, creates a service climate at work, and promotes fairness in the workplace. Employees of servant-leaders are more helping and creative than those working with leaders who score lower on servant leadership. Servant leadership has been shown to be positively related to employee job satisfaction. Servant leadership also has a positive impact on employee commitment to the organization, job performance, and community citizenship behavior. Servant-leaders are good at building and facilitating effective teams. They promote open and problem-driven communication, team confidence, personal integrity, and cooperation among team members.[47]

In addition to expert opinion and scholarly research, we know that there are many companies using servant leadership principles that are doing very well indeed. For example, in 1998, *Fortune* magazine began publishing its list of "The 100 Best Companies to Work for in America." To qualify for the list today, companies must be at least seven years old and have at least 1,000 U.S. employees. Two-thirds of a company's score is based on a 57-question survey which is sent to a minimum of 400 company employees selected on a random basis. The survey asks about attitudes toward management, company philosophy and policies, job satisfaction, and camaraderie in the workplace.

The companies on the *Fortune* list are not only great places to work, they are also high-performance companies that deliver outstanding service and have strong financial returns. The shares of these companies out-perform the stock market, they have low turnover by industry standards, they continue to grow and create new jobs, and they have a bigger talent pool to draw from, because people want to work for them.

Over the years, a number of the top companies on the *Fortune* list have been implementing the principles of servant leadership. Those companies include TDIndustries, Southwest Airlines, Starbucks, Synovus Financial Corporation, Men's Wearhouse, Herman Miller, The Container Store, and AFLAC.

TDIndustries is an air conditioning, construction, and service company based in Dallas. TDIndustries has been implementing servant leadership principals for forty years. The company has been on the 100 Best Companies list for so many years that *Fortune* put the company into its 100 Best Companies "Hall of Fame." Jack Lowe, Jr., who led the company as CEO for twenty-four years, said:

In the past, we believed that being a great place to work would limit our ability to pay top wages, grow our business, and have outstanding financial performance. Our paradigm has shifted. We now believe that being a great place to work *allows* us to pay top wages, grow our business, and have outstanding career opportunities.[48]

Companies that take servant leadership seriously are great places to work, and that is a key element in their success. The ability to attract and keep good people is a strategic business advantage.

Key Practices

The real-world experience of organizations and the testimony of those who have spent decades studying leadership and management tell us that servant leadership really works. But why? Here are some key practices that help explain its effectiveness: self-awareness, listening, changing the pyramid, developing colleagues, coaching instead of controlling, unleashing the energy and intelligence of others, and the use of foresight.

1. Self-Awareness

We need to know what impact we are having on others, so that we can lead them well. As Kouzes and Posner point out in *A Leader's Legacy*, "What's crucial is that you become more self-aware—and self-awareness is a predictor of success in leadership."[49]

Servant-leaders are aware of their strengths and weaknesses. They know that they are not perfect, and yet they can perform at a high level; they know they have their own emotions and biases, and yet they can make wise and fair decisions. By building on their strengths and understanding their weaknesses, they are ready to build on the strengths and understand the weaknesses of others. They are less likely to judge, and more likely to encourage. They appreciate the importance of teams, in which each person is encouraged to contribute his or her strengths to the task at hand. They realize that every person and every job counts, and they treat every employee as a partner and colleague.

Self-awareness includes knowledge of the impact that one's words and deeds have on others. Servant-leaders are aware that saying one thing and doing another can destroy trust. Conversely, being true to your word, even when it is awkward or difficult, can build trust.

One of the hardest things to learn as a leader is that a grimace, an offhand remark, or a joke in poor taste can have a lasting negative impact on others. Conversely, a smile, a thoughtful remark, and an encouraging word can have a lasting positive impact.

Daniel Goleman and his co-authors point out in *Primal Leadership* that people look to the leader for emotional cues. "Emotion" in this sense is about feelings, tone, or mood, as well as strong emotions like happiness or anger. Leaders offer ways to interpret a given situation, and that includes their emotional reactions—the tone or mood of their response. Goleman reported on studies of working groups:

> ... [T]he impact on emotions goes beyond what a leader says. In these studies, even when leaders were not talking, they were watched more carefully than anyone else in the group. When people raised a question for the group as a whole, they would keep their eyes on the leader to see his or her response. Indeed, group members generally see the leader's emotional reaction as the most valid response, and so model their own on it—particularly in an ambiguous situation, where various members react differently. In a sense, the leader sets the emotional standard.[50]

Servant-leaders know that their moods are contagious. A servant-leader who projects a positive mood helps produce enthusiasm and cooperation among team members, which in turn produce success for the team.

Self-awareness arises from reflection. Isabel Lopez, who spent many years in business and then became a teacher of leaders, said:

> ... [O]nly through reflection do we find our purpose and the core of who we are. Reflection enables us to become our own teachers, and we never finish—never finish taking our own class, reading our own book, finding our own heart, and liberating our own spirit. Reflection forces us to face our own lives and beliefs .... Perhaps the greatest gift of reflection is that we ... can find the place that is true for us, the place where passion and serenity meet, both personally and professionally.[51]

Servant-leaders lead from self-awareness, and use the passion, serenity, and wisdom that come from reflection.

2. Listening

Servant-leaders identify and meet the needs of others. The first step toward identifying needs is to listen. Robert Greenleaf said that "only a true natural servant automatically responds to any problem by listening *first*."[52] He told the story of a very able leader who became the head of a large, complex public institution. When the leader realized after a short time that he was not happy with the way things were going, he focused on listening. Greenleaf reported:

> For three months he stopped reading newspapers and listening to news broadcasts; and for this period he relied wholly upon those he met in the course of his work to tell him what was going on. In three months his administrative problems were resolved. No miracles were wrought; but out of sustained intentness of listening that was produced by his unusual decision, this able man learned and received the insights needed to set the right course. And he strengthened his team by so doing.[53]

Servant-leaders gather feedback in as many ways as possible from their colleagues and those they serve. They listen to individuals face to face. They observe what people are doing. They ask questions. They conduct informal interviews, formal interviews, surveys, discussion groups, and focus groups. They use suggestion boxes. They do marketing studies and needs assessments. They are always asking, listening, watching, and thinking about what they learn. This is the foundation of their relevance and effectiveness.

The main point is this: Servant-leaders don't begin with the answer, the program, the product, the procedure, the facility. They don't begin with their own knowledge or expertise. They begin with questions that will help identify the needs of others. What do people say when asked about their needs, their wants, their hopes, their dreams? Servant-leaders watch and listen before they take action. They try hard to identify needs, before they try to meet them.

Taking time to identify needs is moral and respectful. It is also very practical. The simple fact is that *it is very hard to sell a product or service to people who don't want or need it.* If a servant-leader is good at identifying needs, he or she will be in a great position to meet those needs. If the servant-leader does in fact meet those needs, the servant-leader will be effective because he or she will be providing relevant products, programs, and services. That means that the servant-leader's organization will have many satisfied customers, clients, patients, members, or students. The organization will thrive, because the servant-leader listened, and made sure that what the organization offers is what people really *need.*

A problem faced by many organizations is that they are run by people who know a lot. Because they know a lot, they may not have the desire to learn *more.* But if they don't learn more, they simply won't know enough.

One of my favorite examples of this is Muhammad Yunus, who has changed the lives of hundreds of thousands of people in Bangladesh through micro-credit. In his book, *Creating a World without Poverty,* he describes how he was an economics professor, teaching about the nation's long-term plans. He was highly trained—he knew a lot about economic development. But things were not getting better. Finally, he went out into the villages of Bangladesh, and worked with the people, and listened, and discovered what he could do to change the relentless poverty of the country.

What he discovered was that people needed small amounts of capital. They had no collateral, so banks would not loan money to them. But the villagers were willing to work, and the amounts of capital they needed were very small. Yunus started by loaning his own money to people. His first forty-two loans came to a total of U.S. $27. People needed 50 cents or 70 cents to change their lives. Yunus asked for no collateral, but the villagers paid their loans back. He eventually established a bank, and started the mico-credit revolution.

Yunus has continued to watch and listen, and has launched an array of companies, each designed to give opportunities to the poor. It is an amazing story, which began with listening. By the way, the repayment rate over the last 20 years has been 98% to 99%, without collateral. It would have never happened if Yunus had not decided to listen first. He and his bank, Grameen Bank, won the 2006 Nobel Peace Prize for their work, which has spread to other parts of the world. [54]

Servant-leaders know that they have to keep listening, because people and situations change, and soon they can be "mostly right" but not right enough to develop the product or service that people really need. Servant-leaders ask themselves: How much do I really know about the needs of my colleagues and customers? How do I ask, and how often do I ask? Am I really listening? Am I open to hearing things I haven't heard before, as well as things I don't want to hear?

Richard Pieper is the Chairman of PPC Partners, Inc., headquartered in Milwaukee. PPC Partners owns a series of electrical service and construction firms. Dick joined Pieper Electric as President in 1960, when the family-owned business had eight employees doing $250,000 of business per year. Today, PPC Partners, Inc. employs 900 to 1,100 people, has sales in the hundreds of millions, and is one of the top electrical contracting firms in the United States.

One reason for the company's dramatic growth is that company leaders are good at getting feedback from colleagues and customers. They are always asking and listening. After every company semi-annual briefing, those who attended are asked to fill out an evaluation form that asks about the attendees' overall reaction to the meeting, pre-meeting communications, transportation, hotel, meeting room, food service (each meal), the program, and the chairman. They are asked what they enjoyed the most, and the least; what they learned and intend to implement; and what they recommend for future meetings. For regular meetings, there is a two-page "Post Meeting Reaction" form that asks similar questions. Dick even has a Chairman's Office Survey in which he asks each employee to rate him and his executive assistant on their quality of service, reliability, knowledge, and timeliness. Then, of course, there are regular surveys of customers. The comments are studied, and follow-up is comprehensive. At PPC Partners, listening is a high priority. It is a broad-based, systematic process with a focus on constant follow-up and improvement.

Part of the listening process consists of testing products or services in their early stages of development, to make sure they are aligned with customer needs. Years ago, when developing a new four-wheel, all-terrain vehicle (ATV), Suzuki Motor Company engineers took prototypes of the ATV to the apple orchards of Washington and asked the workers to try them out. The engineers watched and listened to the feedback they got from these early users. For example, the workers said they needed a basket for tools and insecticides, so the engineers added a basket.

Then they took the prototype to a local Suzuki dealer. He rode off, and was away a long time. The engineers began to worry. Did he have an accident? Did the prototype break down? Finally the manager returned with a big smile on his face. "That was fun!" he said. "I want to order twenty of these." It was only after listening and testing that the engineers knew that their product was ready to market.

3. Changing the Pyramid

The traditional organizational hierarchy is a pyramid. There are a few people at the top—the people who have power. Then there are more people in the middle, often known as middle managers. Most of the people are at the base of the pyramid. These are the people who create and deliver the products, programs, and services that the organization provides.

After 38 years of work at AT&T, Greenleaf concluded that the pyramidal structure doesn't work. In his essay, *The Institution as Servant,* he wrote:

> To be a lone chief atop a pyramid is *abnormal and corrupting.* None of us are perfect by ourselves, and all of us need the help and correcting influence of close colleagues. When someone is moved atop a pyramid, that person no longer has colleagues, only subordinates. Even the frankest and bravest of subordinates do not talk with their boss in the same way that they talk with colleagues who are equals, and normal communication patterns become warped .... The pyramidal structure weakens informal links, dries up channels of honest reaction and feedback, and creates limiting chief-subordinate relationships which, at the top, can seriously penalize the whole organization.

A self-protective *image of omniscience* often evolves from these warped and filtered communications. This in time defeats any leader by causing a distortion of judgment, for one's judgment is often best sharpened through interaction with others who are free to challenge and criticize.

Those persons who are atop the pyramids often suffer from a very real *loneliness*. They cannot be sure enough of the motives of those with whom they must deal, and they are not on the grapevine. Most of what they know is what other people choose to tell them. They often do not know what everybody else knows, informally.[55]

One solution is to broaden the top of the pyramid. Greenleaf recommended that organizations be led by teams in which the leader is not the boss but *primus inter pares*, or "first among equals."

Primus inter pares was the leadership model for universities founded in medieval Europe, at which faculty members gathered and elected one of their own as leader. The leader was expected to preside and guide as the equal of those who elected him. This ideal of collegial leadership is cherished by many faculty today.

I truly enjoyed being *primus inter pares* while chairing three accreditation teams in higher education. The teams consisted of accomplished professionals from different academic institutions who had university experience in a variety of areas such as academic programs, finance, information technology, student services, and governance. We would gather on the campus we were sent to evaluate, share our questions or concerns, and make plans. During the next two days, we would divide up and conduct individual meetings with faculty, students, staff, and administrators; research specific questions; and then reconvene to share what we had learned. Each member of the team would draft his or her own observations and conclusions, which I would compile into a single report. It was a "self-regulating" group that did not need a "boss." My role was to be the convener, the presider, the facilitator, and at the end of our visit, the spokesperson for the team.

One of the problems with the traditional pyramidal structure is that workers focus on pleasing their "bosses." Unfortunately, you can please your boss, and she can please hers, and he can please the board of directors, while nobody is really focused on *pleasing the customer*. When the pyramid is inverted, or tipped on its side, everyone in the organization can focus on pleasing customers, clients, members, or participants—the people whom the organization is designed to serve, and the people who will ultimately decide if the organization succeeds.

Bill Turner, who led the teams that built a number of companies, including Synovus Financial Corporation, said this:

> Based on the tenet that servant leadership is a commitment to love and serve, the organizational structure is turned upside down, with the leader at the bottom of the hierarchy, supporting those who do the work. The leader's primary responsibility is to meet the needs, whatever they may be, of those who serve the organization. It involves listening to others and together shaping a vision that everyone can own. The servant-leader becomes a funnel that creative ideas come to naturally from others who are themselves becoming servant-leaders. Servant-leaders are encouragers, communicators, and cheerleaders.[56]

Ken Blanchard, in his book *Leading at a Higher Level*, pointed out that servant-leaders stand at the top of the pyramid only when articulating the mission and vision of the organization, so everyone will know what direction the organization is going. After servant-leaders have listened and set the direction, their role changes. Blanchard said:

> Once people are clear on where they are going, the leader's role shifts to a service mindset for the task of implementation—the second aspect of leadership. How do you make the dream happen? *Implementation is where the servant aspect of servant leadership comes into play* .... Servant-leaders ... feel that their role is to help people achieve their goals. They constantly try to find out what their people need to perform well and live according to the vision.[57]

Steven B. Sample, former President of the University of Southern California, told a story in his book, *The Contrarian's Guide to Leadership*. At the tender age of thirty, he was named deputy director for academic affairs of the Illinois Board of Higher Education. The board's chairman, George Clements, was a successful business man.

Sample recalled that when he started work, Mr. Clements advised him to spend only 10 percent of his time hiring, evaluating, exhorting, praising, and motivating the people who reported directly to him. Clements said: "For the remaining 90 percent of your time you should be doing *everything you can* to help your direct reports succeed. You should be the first assistant to the people who work for you."[58] Clements told Sample to "work for those who work for you!" Sample has found this advice to be very valuable. He said:

> If you're not in the process of getting rid of a lieutenant, bend over backwards to help him get his job done. That means returning his phone calls promptly, listening carefully to his plans and problems, calling on others at his request, and helping him formulate his goals and develop strategies for achieving those goals. It's not simply that you should be your lieutenant's staff person, you should be his *best* staff person.[59]

In *The Servant Leader,* James Autry puts it this way: "One of the primary functions of the manager/leader is to assure that people get the resources they need to do the job. To be a leader who serves, you must think of yourself as—and indeed must be—their principal resource."[60]

4. Developing Your Colleagues

Greenleaf's best test of the servant-leader was: "Do those served grow as persons? Do they, *while being served*, become healthier, wiser, freer, more autonomous, more likely themselves to become servants?[61] Those served include one's colleagues. Helping them grow is a triple win: When your colleagues grow, the capacity of your organization grows, and the ability of your organization to serve others grows.

In his essay on "Servant Leadership in Business," Greenleaf proposed a new business ethic:

> Looking at the two major elements, the work and the person, the new ethic, simply but quite completely stated, will be: *the work exists for the person as much as the person exists for the work.* To put it another way, the business exists as much to provide meaningful work to the person as it exists to produce a product or service to the customer.

.... When the business manager who is fully committed to this ethic is asked, 'What are you in business for?'" the answer may be: '*I am in the business of growing people* .... Incidentally, we also make and sell at a profit things that people want to buy so that we can pay for all this.'[62]

The TDIndustries "Mission Statement" is built on this ethic. The statement says: "We are committed to providing outstanding career opportunities by exceeding our customers' expectations through continuous aggressive improvement." The Mission Statement is elaborated by saying, "We believe in continuous, intense 'people-development' efforts, including substantial training budgets." The worker is as important as the work.

The Schneider Corporation in Indianapolis grew dramatically after it adopted servant leadership as a business philosophy twenty years ago. In its vision statement, the company sets forth its commitment to "challenging, encouraging and supporting one another so that we all grow personally and professionally." The company believes that servant leadership is a journey, and "servant-leaders are responsible for helping grow every person with whom they interact along their journey."

Since adults spend most of their waking hours at work, their workplaces have a huge impact on their personal growth and the meaning they find in life. Organizations have an ethical duty to provide workers with the opportunity to grow and find meaning. That is why servant-leaders offer learning experiences in the form of mentoring, training, new assignments, well-timed promotions, and broad-based experience in the organization. They keep track of the developmental needs and opportunities of their colleagues.

In *The Effective Executive*, Peter Drucker told the story of a company president whose contribution was the development of young managers at a large chain of retail stores. He was a "financial man" who had faithfully served in the number two slot in the company. When the CEO suddenly died, he became the new president. Even though he preferred working with numbers, he concluded that he could make the biggest difference by developing the company's managers. So three times a week he walked through the personnel department after lunch and picked up eight or ten file folders at random—the folders of young managers. Drucker reported:

> Back in his office, he opened the first man's folder, scanned it
> rapidly, and put through a telephone call to the man's superior. 'Mr.
> Robertson, this is the president in New York. You have on your staff
> a young man, Joe Jones. Didn't you recommend six months ago
> that he be put in a job where he could acquire some merchandising
> experience? You did. Why haven't you done anything about it?' And
> down would go the receiver.[63]

The president also called to congratulate supervisors for making sure that
their young managers got the experience they needed to continue growing.
Drucker said: "This man was in the president's chair only a few years
before he himself retired. But today, ten or fifteen years later, executives
who never met him attribute to him, and with considerable justice, the
tremendous growth and success of the company since his time." He simply
focused on developing people.[64]

The servant-leader takes great pleasure in helping others to grow and
become all that they can be. Stu Gothold was the Superintendent of the
Los Angeles County Schools, responsible for 4,000 employees and 1.6
million students in 82 districts. "I feel good when I help others succeed,"
Stu says. He likes a consensus style of decision-making. "I want to spend
time on a problem or topic, and give people the chance to get their
arms around it, so everyone has a piece of it," he says. "I want to make
sure I hear from the people who are working directly with the kids." He
acknowledges everybody as a member of the team. The reward of being
the team leader is seeing the achievements of all the team members.
"Years later, people still stay in touch," Stu says. "That has made it all
even more rewarding. I still hear from former students and colleagues."

Servant-leaders know that the mission of the organization is bigger
than any one person. By developing their colleagues, servant-leaders
improve not only the organization's performance today, but far into the
future. That is the servant-leader's legacy: A strong, vibrant team that is
trained and ready to take on any challenge, come what may.

5. Coaching, Not Controlling

In the power model, and many management textbooks, the assumption is that a leader or manager exercises power to "control" his or her unit or organization. The people who report to the manager constitute his or her "span of control." The manager's job is to "keep things under control."

James Showkeir is an organizational development expert who assists organizations in implementing servant leadership. He said: "The traditional belief is that, for the organization to succeed, organizational power should be entrusted to only a few at the top of the organization. The rest of the organization should comply with their directions and suffer the bureaucracy, even if it inhibits serving the customers."[65] A high price is paid for this kind of compliance. Showkeir pointed out:

> Compliance is not commitment. Compliance does not create passion. Compliance does not make individuals wiser. Compliance does not encourage choosing accountability. Compliance does not lead to creativity, flexibility, differentiation, and speed. Compliance does not create meaning and purpose. Compliance does not breed freedom. Meaning, purpose, and freedom ensue from struggle, risk, and engagement; compliance cuts us away from these.[66]

Servant-leaders are not focused on controlling their "subordinates." They do not measure their status in terms of their "span of control." They are not focused on compliance. Instead, they are focused on coaching and mentoring.

Kouzes and Posner note: "The more you control others, the more likely it is that they will rebel. Exemplary leaders have repeatedly told us that they get the greatest commitment precisely when they let their people go."[67] People do their best when they are taught, mentored, and coached, benefiting from both positive and negative feedback as they make their daily decisions and do their daily work.

In *The Servant Leader,* James Autry listed the six things he believes about leadership:

1. Leadership is not about controlling people; it's about caring for people and being a useful resource for people.

2. Leadership is not about being boss; it's about being present for people and building a community at work.

3. Leadership is not about holding on to territory; it's about letting go of ego, bringing your spirit to work, being your best and most authentic self.

4. Leadership is less concerned with pep talks and more concerned with creating a place in which people can do good work, can find meaning in their work, and can bring their spirits to work.

5. Leadership, like life, is largely a matter of paying attention.

6. Leadership requires love.[68]

Herb Kelleher, the former CEO of Southwest Airlines, said: "I have always believed that the best leader is the best server. And if you're a servant, by definition, you're not controlling."[69]

One reason that servant-leaders don't focus on controlling others is that *nobody really controls anybody else.* Each of us controls our own time and attention, but nobody else's. Yes, leaders can threaten, or persuade, or plead, but individuals have to decide if they are going to cooperate and respond to their leaders. Leaders may have "authority," but their followers have to accept and respond to that authority, or nothing will happen.

That was the message delivered by Chester Barnard back in the late 1930s. Barnard was a Bell Telephone executive, a man who knew something about business, education, government, and philanthropic organizations. In *The Functions of the Executive*, he argued that authority rests in the hands of the *receiver* of a communication. He said:

The necessity of the assent of the individual to establish authority for him is inescapable. A person can and will accept a communication as authoritative only when four conditions simultaneously obtain: *(a)* he can and does understand the communication; *(b) at the time of his decision* he believes that it is not inconsistent with the purpose of the organization; *(c) at the time of his decision,* he believes it to be compatible with his personal interest as a whole; and *(d)* he is able mentally and physically to comply with it.[70]

For the leader, then, giving orders is not enough. People need to understand, see the purpose, be in personal alignment, and be willing and able to do what is requested. You can't *make* them do that.

Servant-leaders know that people are not only capable of resisting an order—they are free to leave the organization and find a job somewhere else. Jack Lowe, Jr. of TDIndustries points out: "Your best employees have the talent and ability to leave your company and find work elsewhere if they want to. So you should lead them the way you lead volunteers."[71]

In addition to the difficulty of controlling people, a leader cannot control the organization's results through rigid organizational structures. One of the insights offered by Margaret Wheatley in *Leadership and the New Science* is that the universe can no longer best be understood as a machine, as in Newtonian physics. Rather, it is best understood in terms of relationships and connections, as in quantum physics. In mechanistic models, disruptions are seen as trouble. But in the new science, disorder can lead to new life and higher forms of order.

We should no longer expect our organizations to operate as machines we can control, but as dynamic living systems in which we can participate. We can lead by influencing and responding to the changes around us. We can support the emergence of new kinds of order that will work for us and our organizations. Servant-leaders thrive in an environment in which constant adjustment is necessary, because they are good at listening and identifying the changing needs.

The issue for the servant-leader is not how to control others, but how to build strong, positive relationships with others. Wheatley said:

> To live in a quantum world, to weave here and there with ease
> and grace, we will need to change what we do. We will need to
> stop describing tasks and instead facilitate process. We will need
> to become savvy about how to build relationships, how to nurture
> growing, evolving things. All of us will need better skills in listening,
> communicating, and facilitating groups, because these are the talents
> that build strong relationships .... Those who relate through coercion,
> or from a disregard for the other person, create negative energy.
> Those who are open to others and who see others in their fullness

create positive energy. Love in organizations, then, is the most potent source of power we have available.[72]

Servant leaders participate, guide, coach, and facilitate. They lead by identifying new sources of order and creating positive energy in their relationships.

6. Unleashing the Energy and Intelligence of Others

After developing and coaching their colleagues, servant-leaders encourage their colleagues to make more decisions on their own. Servant-leaders develop and coach their colleagues so that their colleagues will use their energy and intelligence wisely, for the good of the organization and those the organization serves.

Unleashing the energy and intelligence of others is a competitive advantage. As Stephen Covey said:

> You've got to produce more for less, and with greater speed than you've ever done before. The only way you can do that in a sustained way is through the empowerment of people. And the only way you get empowerment is through high-trust cultures and through the empowerment philosophy that turns bosses into servants and coaches .... Leaders are learning that this kind of empowerment, which is what servant leadership represents, is one of *the* key principles that, based on practice, not talk, will be the deciding point between an organization's enduring success or its eventual extinction.[73]

The importance of empowering cuts across different types of organizations. For example, Dan Ebener has conducted research on the impact of servant leadership at high-performing Catholic parishes. He focused on three servant leadership behaviors—recognizing, serving, and empowering. "Recognizing" includes acknowledging, affirming, and calling forth the gifts and talents of parishioners. "Serving" includes putting the needs and interests of others first. "Empowering" means involving the followers in making decisions that affect their own roles and goals within the organization. Ebener found that each of these behaviors, especially empowering leadership behaviors, supported high performance.[74] Servant leadership worked well at the parishes he studied.

Jack Lowe, Sr. founded Texas Distributors (now TDIndustries) in Dallas in 1946. When Greenleaf published his essay, *The Servant as Leader,* in 1970, Jack Lowe got a copy—and then bought more and more copies, sharing them in his company and throughout the community. Greenleaf called to find out why Lowe was buying so many copies, and that began a friendship between the two men. Lowe held discussion groups with employees to talk about Greenleaf's essay and how they might apply it at Texas Distributors. Out of those discussions grew a list of leadership values, including:

- Leaders are first a servant of those they lead. They are a teacher, a source of information and knowledge and a standard setter, more than a giver of directions and a disciplinarian.

- Leaders see things through the eyes of their followers. They put themselves in others' shoes and help them make their dreams come true.

- Leaders assume that their followers are working with them. They consider others Partners in the work and see to it that they share in the rewards. They glorify the team spirit!

- Leaders are people builders. They help those around them to grow because the leader realizes that the more strong people an organization has, the stronger it will be.

- Leaders do not hold people down, they lift them up. They reach out their hand to help their followers scale the peaks.

- Leaders have faith in people. They believe in them. They have found that others rise to their high expectations.

- Leaders can be led. They are not interested in having their own way, but in finding the best way. They have an open mind.[75]

These leadership values are about unleashing the energy and intelligence of everyone in the company.

Sometimes, a Partner at TDIndustries is not aligned with the company's values, and has to be asked to leave. One of the leadership values of the company states:

- Leaders are faced with many hard decisions, including balancing fairness to an individual with fairness to the group. This sometimes requires a 'weeding out' of those in the group who, over a period of time, do not measure up to the group needs of dependability, productivity and safety.

The hard decision has to be made, so that all Partners will be able to work well together in meeting the needs of customers.

Not unleashing the energy and intelligence of others is extraordinarily sad and wasteful. Most people work in service industries and perform knowledge work that requires individual decisions and judgments. Knowledge and skill are needed at all levels, and everyone counts. It doesn't make any sense to have lots of people in an organization, but let only a few people—those at the top—use their full potential. The people at the top of the pyramid can't *know* everything or *do* everything. They are only human; they have limits. Without participation and input from colleagues throughout the organization, they will make mistakes. Customers will be lost. Opportunities to develop new products and services will be lost.

In most organizations today, people are the biggest asset. The organization is paying for *all* its people. Why not engage them fully in the work at hand? Full engagement makes the organization more competitive, because it deploys more of its resources. The organization will be better able to understand and respond to the needs of colleagues and customers. Encouraging the full engagement of every member of the organization is also respectful: It shows confidence in the knowledge and skill of others. It sends a positive, inspiring message to those who interact with customers and make thousands of decisions each day that affect the future of the organization.

As James Showkeir pointed out, "the major problem with the traditional system is that it consolidates organizational power in places that have the least marketplace and customer contact. *Those with the most contact are the least powerful.*"[76] The energy and intelligence of those with the most contact must be unleashed for the organization to achieve its greatest possible success.

Howard Behar was one of the senior leaders who helped build Starbucks from twenty-eight stores to thousands of stores worldwide. He says that organizations should empower people to bring their unique perspectives and skills to the job. Leaders should also remember that those closest to the job are likely to have the best understanding of how to get the job done. "After all," Behar asks, "who is better equipped to choose the broom than the guy who sweeps the floor?"[77]

One way to unleash energy and intelligence is to build upon the intrinsic motivation of colleagues. Research done by Dr. Kenneth Thomas on motivation at work suggests that a sense of choice is a key intrinsic motivator.[78] A servant-leader who gives colleagues choices regarding the way they accomplish their work can unleash their intrinsic motivation. This is important, because research shows that people who are intrinsically motivated are more productive, more committed, more innovative, and less likely to burn out. According to Kouzes and Posner in their book, *The Leadership Challenge*, "external motivation is more likely to create conditions of compliance or defiance; self-motivation produces far superior results."[79]

Ken Melrose provides a good example of how to unleash the energy and intelligence of others. Melrose helped unleash his colleagues at Game Time, a subsidiary of the Toro Company that manufactured playground equipment. In 1973, at the age of thirty-two, Melrose was hired to lead the company.

The previous CEO was the founder of the company, and he made all the decisions. So when Melrose became president, the staff came to him, asking him questions and expecting *him* to make all the decisions. He declined. Instead, he asked them questions. If the staff member wanted to know how much steel to purchase, Melrose would ask him how much they bought in the last period, and how many merry-go-rounds they built with that amount of steel, and how many merry-go-rounds the sales manager thought they could sell in the next period, and how many merry-go-rounds they already had in stock, and so forth. He didn't tell them to do it on their own, and he didn't give them his own answer. Instead, he coached them with the questions until they could see how to work out the answers for themselves. Melrose recalled:

Over the three years I worked at Game Time, much of my effort was spent helping people learn processes for problem solving and decision making related to their jobs .... Bit by bit, I came to understand that you lead best by serving the needs of your people. You don't do their jobs for them; you enable them to learn and progress on the job. You multiply strengths as you empower and trust.[80]

During those three years, people began to enjoy their jobs. They had more confidence, more trust in each other, and they experienced better team work. Their sales increased 50 percent, their profits more than doubled, and Game Time was yielding the best return on investment of all of Toro's divisions. Later, in the early eighties, when the parent company was about to collapse, the board asked Melrose to become the CEO of all of Toro. He applied servant leadership principles in rebuilding and growing the company during the next twenty-two years.

7. Foresight

Greenleaf said that the central ethic of leadership is foresight. He said that "prescience, or foresight, is a better than average guess about *what* is going to happen *when* in the future."[81] Greenleaf said that a good leader has a high level of intuitive insight about the way the past and the present connect to the future. The servant-leader is "in every moment of time, historian, contemporary analyst, and prophet—not three separate roles."[82] Greenleaf said:

Foresight is the 'lead' that the leader has. Once leaders lose this lead and events start to force their hand, they are leaders in name only. They are not leading, but are reacting to immediate events, and they probably will not long be leaders. There are abundant current examples of loss of leadership which stem from a failure to foresee what reasonably could have been foreseen, and from failure to act on that knowledge while the leader had freedom to act.[83]

Greenleaf said that the failure of a leader to foresee events may be viewed as an *ethical* failure, because a failure of foresight can put an organization in a bad situation that might have been avoided. Organizations tend to behave unethically when they are backed into a corner, and feel that they have no choices left except bad ones. Allowing an organization to get into that situation is itself an ethical failure.

Daniel Kim, an organizational consultant who has worked with America's largest corporations, distinguished between forecasting and foresight. He said:

> It would seem ... that the enormous complexity of our modern organizations leaves us incapable of exercising foresight, thereby sentencing us to be ethical failures as leaders. This would be true if we equated foresight with making accurate forecasts about the future (which is impossible to do). Fortunately for us, foresight is about being able to perceive the *significance and nature of events* before they have occurred (which is achievable).[84]

Kim shared an example used by Arie de Geus of Royal Dutch Shell:

> If it rains in the foothills of the Himalayas, we cannot forecast exactly when the rivers will swell and flood the valleys, but we can predict with certainty that the flooding will occur. The better we know the structure of the terrain, the greater knowledge we have about the flooding to follow. An ethical responsibility of a leader is to know the underlying structures within her domain of responsibility and be able to make predictions that can guide her people to a better future.[85]

Today, many leaders serve as CEOs for no more than a few years before retiring or moving to another position. As a result, many leaders are tempted to go for short-term gains, while ignoring long-term issues. They assume that they will be gone before the long-term issues become important, so they exercise little foresight. Unfortunately, the people who are still working in the organization, and those they serve, will suffer the disadvantages of the CEO's failure of foresight when the long-term issues become the central issues—or crises—years later.

Even when CEOs stay for the long term, they can fail to use foresight, and their organizations can suffer dismal consequences. In his book *Good to Great,* Jim Collins compared the Great Atlantic and Pacific Tea Company, known as A&P, with the Kroger grocery chain. In the 1950s, A&P was the largest retailing organization in the world, while Kroger was only about half as large. Both companies were old, both had nearly all their assets invested in traditional grocery stores, and both knew that the world was changing. In fact, both experimented with a new kind of "superstore."

However, fifty years later, A&P had faded away, and Kroger had pulled far ahead. The difference was that Kroger had foresight, and acted on it. Kroger concluded from its superstore experiment that the traditional grocery store would become extinct in the future. Kroger therefore eliminated, changed, or replaced every store and rebuilt its entire system on the new superstore model. By 1999, after years of spectacular growth, it had become the number one grocery chain in the United States.[86]

According to Noel Tichy and Warren Bennis in their book, *Judgment: How Winning Leaders Make Great Calls*, good judgment calls about the future are essential, and they require foresight. For example, in deciding where to lead General Electric in the future, CEO Jeff Immelt analyzed social, economic, and environmental trends and then began deciding what products or services to produce. Tichy and Bennis report that Immelt built his strategy on the assumption that the economy may grow more slowly and be more volatile; that to attract and motivate good people, GE will need to be more humane; and that GE can generate organic growth by using its research and technology base to develop new markets. Some of those markets will be in developing countries that need infrastructure, while in more advanced economies the opportunities are most likely to be in health care, in energy saving and production, and in environmentally friendly products.[87] Foresight in these areas became the basis for GE's business decisions for the future.

Joseph Jaworski led the scenario planning process at Royal Dutch Shell in the early 1990s. Shell had 120,000 employees in more than one hundred countries. Jaworski assembled a team to build the scenarios, and met with the company's most senior managers. As the process moved forward, it became clear that the global scenarios for the next thirty years would have to address the relationship between rich and poor countries. Two scenarios were finally developed—a pessimistic scenario they called "Barricades," which described an increasingly divided world with increased anarchy, and a more optimistic one they called "New Frontiers," which featured political and economic freedom for people around the world.

Jaworski observed that developing and sharing the scenarios changed the perceptions of those involved. In fact, rather than using the scenarios to react to events in the world when they occur, understanding the scenarios influenced how some people behaved *in advance of those events*. Jaworski concluded: "If individuals and organizations operate from the generative orientation, from possibility rather than resignation, we can *create* the future into which we are living, as opposed to merely reacting to it when we get there."[88] Exercising foresight can do more than prepare us for the future—it can help us create the future that we desire the most.

I had the honor and pleasure of serving in the cabinet of Hawaii Governor George Ariyoshi, a true public servant. Governor Ariyoshi was not only concerned about serving his community today—he worked hard to take into account future generations. He spent much of his time as a public servant trying to make life better for those who will come after us. His efforts were not focused on getting votes, because those who would most appreciate his efforts were not even born yet. His efforts were focused instead on creating our "preferred future." The interesting thing is that he was in political life for thirty years and never lost an election. People trusted him. People who met him and came to know him understood that he wasn't in it for himself, he was in it for the long-term good of the community.

Leaders with foresight can provide and maintain momentum in their organizations. This is something that leaders owe their colleagues and those they serve. In *Leadership Is an Art,* Max De Pree said:

> Leadership comes with a lot of debts to the future .... Momentum is one. Momentum in a vital company is palpable. It is not abstract or mysterious. It is the feeling among a group of people that their lives and work are intertwined and moving toward a recognizable and legitimate goal .... Momentum comes from a clear vision of what the corporation ought to be, from a well-thought-out strategy to achieve that vision, and from carefully conceived and communicated directions and plans which enable everyone to participate and be publicly accountable in achieving those plans.[89]

Leaders hold the future of their colleagues and customers in their hands. Foresight is needed to form the vision, create the plans, and generate the momentum that will make that future a good one for everyone.

5.

The Meaningful Lives
of Servant-Leaders

Why do people become servant-leaders? It may be that they have a natural desire to serve, or it may be that they hear the call as a result of their life experience. They spend years focused on their personal ambitions for power, wealth, and fame, and discover that such things are empty and meaningless compared with simple acts of service. It may be a result of their faith—they seek to follow the teachings of their religion. It may be that they love people, and simply want to help them. Whatever the case may be, they are committed to serving others.

That commitment is important, because servant-leaders are not always successful. Things may not go the way they had hoped, or people may not appreciate what they have done, or people may even criticize them for the good they are trying to do. But servant-leaders continue to help, no matter how difficult it may be.

Servant-leaders do not work to earn the appreciation of others. Appreciation may come their way, but it is not what motivates them. They derive a sense of meaning and satisfaction from doing a great job. It doesn't matter whether anybody else knows or appreciates what they do— *they* know. And that's enough.

Each of us likes to be appreciated. That's normal. But it is hard to be a servant-leader if you crave applause. Focusing on applause means that you are focused on yourself, not others. Servant-leaders focus instead on the meaning and satisfaction that they receive when they help others. That is something that nobody can take away from them. The meaning and satisfaction are theirs, whether anybody else applauds or not.

I was fortunate to learn this early in life. One of the real "aha!" experiences of my life occurred as I walked to the stadium for the student awards ceremony at my high school. It occurred to me that I was so happy about what I had done that year, and felt so good about what I had learned, and whom I had helped, that I didn't need any awards. *I had already been rewarded.* I already had the sense of meaning and satisfaction that came from doing a good job. That realization was a major breakthrough for me. I felt liberated. I felt an immense inner peace.

A couple of years later I was in college. It was the 1960s, a time of conflict and confrontation on many American college campuses. It was also a time of hope and high ideals. What disturbed me the most was watching idealistic young people go out into the world to do what they thought was right and good and true, only to come back a short time later, discouraged, or even embittered, because they didn't achieve the change they sought to achieve, or nobody seemed to appreciate what they were trying to do.

I was working with student leaders back then, and I had two basic messages for them. First, I told them that you really have to love people. You have to really care, because change usually takes time, and love is one of the only motivations that is strong enough to keep you with the people and with the process until change is achieved. The second message was this: If you go out into the world and do what you believe is right and good and true, then you will get a lot of meaning and satisfaction. If people appreciate you, that's fine, but if they don't, that's okay. *If you have the meaning, you don't have to have the glory.*

The Paradoxical Commandments

In my sophomore year in college, when I was 19, I wrote a booklet for high school student leaders. In that booklet I urged them to learn how to work with others to get things done. I challenged them with what I called "The Paradoxical Commandments of Leadership." This is what I wrote:

1. People are illogical, unreasonable, and self-centered.
   Love them anyway.

2. If you do good, people will accuse you of selfish ulterior motives.
   Do good anyway.

3. If you are successful, you will win false friends and true enemies.
   Succeed anyway.

4. The good you do today will be forgotten tomorrow.
   Do good anyway.

5. Honesty and frankness make you vulnerable.
   Be honest and frank anyway.

6. The biggest men and women with the biggest ideas can be shot down
   by the smallest men and women with the smallest minds.
   Think big anyway.

7. People favor underdogs but follow only top dogs.
   Fight for a few underdogs anyway.

8. What you spend years building may be destroyed overnight.
   Build anyway.

9. People really need help but may attack you if you do help them.
   Help people anyway.

10. Give the world the best you have and you'll get kicked in the teeth.
    Give the world the best you have anyway.[90]

The Paradoxical Commandments are guidelines for finding personal
meaning in the face of adversity. That's why the first phrase in each
commandment is about adversity, or difficulty, or disappointment: People
are illogical, unreasonable, and self-centered. The good you do today will
be forgotten tomorrow. People really need help, but may attack you if you
do help them.

But each statement about adversity is followed by a positive
commandment: Love people anyway. Do good anyway. Help people
anyway.

The paradox is this. Even when the world is difficult—even when
the world is *crazy*—you and I can still find personal meaning and deep
happiness. We do that by facing the worst in the world with the best in
ourselves.

The fact is that you and I, as individuals, can't control the external world. We can't control the world economy, and the rate of population growth. We can't control the weather, or natural disasters like fires and floods. We can't control when terrorists may strike or wars may break out. We can't control which companies will acquire which companies, and which jobs will be downsized and which jobs will open up. We can work hard, and prepare, and seize opportunities—and we should. We can join with others to influence those external events—and we should do that, too. But there are lots of things in our external world we just can't control.

What we can control is our inner lives. You and I get to decide who we are going to be and how we are going to live. We can live our most cherished values, and be close to our families and friends, and do what we know is right and good and true—no matter what. *No matter what.* The good news is that these are the things that have been giving people a lot of personal meaning for thousands of years.

Servant-leaders understand the Paradoxical Commandments. The Paradoxical Commandments focus on personal meaning, and so do servant-leaders. That is what makes it possible for them to keep working, whether they get applause, indifference, or even a negative response. They like to be treated well, but they are not especially concerned when they are treated badly. Servant-leaders are not worried about the attention others pay to them, but the attention they pay to others. That's where the meaning is to be found.

Meaning Is an Intrinsic Motivator

Finding meaning is important, because personal meaning is an intrinsic motivator. People are intrinsically motivated when they do something because they want to, not because they have to. They are intrinsically motivated when their work is interesting, and fulfilling, and meaningful. Research and common sense tell us that people who are intrinsically motivated are more productive, more innovative, more committed, and less likely to burn out than those who are extrinsically motivated. Since servant-leaders are intrinsically motivated, they have a big advantage over power-oriented leaders, who are extrinsically motivated.

Extrinsic motivation applies when people are motivated by something other than the work or activity itself. For example, a person who does her job not because she likes it, but as a way to get power or money, is extrinsically motivated.

Extrinsic rewards will always be important. We need to provide for ourselves and our families, so we care about salaries, benefits, bonuses, and awards. That's normal. But we want more than that, and need more than that, if we are to be productive, innovative, committed, and energized. We need to be intrinsically motivated.

Dr. Kenneth Thomas, who has done a great deal of research on motivation at work, points out:

> ... [S]tudies show that the intrinsic rewards are consistently related to job satisfaction and to performance. These findings hold across types of organizations and for managers as well as workers. Studies have also shown that the intrinsic rewards are related to innovativeness, commitment to the organization, and reduced stress.[91]

A sense of meaningfulness is an important intrinsic motivator at work. It is also very fundamental to our nature as human beings. Thomas said:

> There is a great deal of evidence that people are hardwired to care about purposes. We seem to need to see ourselves as going somewhere—as being on a journey in pursuit of a significant purpose .... There is also much evidence that people suffer when they lack purpose. Clinical studies show that people deteriorate in various ways without purpose.[92]

Dramatic testimony on this point came from Viktor Frankl in his book, *Man's Search for Meaning*. Frankl was a Jewish psychiatrist who survived the Nazi concentration camps in World War II. His story of life as a prisoner is a painful story of suffering and death. Prisoners had to work hard each day, with little food, clothing, sleep, or medicine in an environment of constant brutality and fear. Frankl observed that prisoners who had faith in the future, who still had a reason to live, were the ones who were most likely to survive. From this experience, he developed his theory of logotherapy, or meaning therapy, in which a patient is confronted with and reoriented toward the meaning of his life. Frankl believed that "striving to find a meaning in one's life is the primary motivational force in man."[93] That meaning varies from person to person, because each person's circumstances and tasks are different.

Bill Turner led the team that built Synovus Financial into the #1 Best Place to Work in America on the *Fortune* magazine list for 1999. In his book, *The Learning of Love: A Journey Toward Servant Leadership*, Turner mentioned many times his own search for meaning. Listening to Viktor Frankl lecture and reading his book, *Man's Search for Meaning*, were on Turner's list of experiences that shaped his life. Turner filled the emptiness in his soul with his faith, his love and compassion, and the meaning he derived from serving others.

Meaning Is Good for Mental Health

In addition to being more productive, more committed, more innovative, and less likely to burn out, people who are intrinsically motivated are also psychologically healthier.

Edward L. Deci wrote a book titled, *Why We Do What We Do: Understanding Self Motivation*. The book included a report on a study done on six types of life aspirations. Three were extrinsic—the aspiration to be wealthy, famous, and physically attractive. The other three were intrinsic—the aspiration to have meaningful personal relationships, to make contributions to the community, and to grow as individuals. Deci said:

> ... [S]trong aspirations for any of the intrinsic goals ... were positively associated with well-being. People who strongly desired to contribute to their community, for example, had more vitality and higher self-esteem. When people organize their behavior in terms of intrinsic strivings (relative to extrinsic strivings) they seem more content—they feel better about who they are and display more evidence of psychological health.[94]

The extrinsic goals were about what one *has*. The intrinsic goals were about who one *is*. The research showed that people who were heavily focused on extrinsic rewards had poor mental health.

This makes sense. If your goals are extrinsic, reaching them depends on the decisions of others and whims of fate over which you have no control. By contrast, reaching your intrinsic goals depends on your attitude, your values, and your work. Servant-leaders are focused on the intrinsic goal of identifying and meeting the needs of others. As a result, they have better mental health than many other kinds of leaders.

Meaning Is a Key to Deep Happiness

There is no question that finding personal meaning in life is also a key to being deeply happy. What do I mean by "deep happiness"? I mean the kind of happiness that touches your spirit and connects with your soul. It is hard to describe. Some people call it joy, or self-fulfillment, or self-actualization, or being centered. Others call it living their passion, or following their bliss. For people of faith, it may be finding the divine will for their lives, and then living that will. But however we describe it, personal meaning is a key.

In his book *Happiness: Lessons from a New Science,* Richard Layard stated that "people who achieve a sense of meaning in their lives are happier than those who live from one pleasure to another."[95] Layard quoted a study that showed that other factors that correlate with happiness and life satisfaction are autonomy, positive relationships, personal growth and self-acceptance.

Dennis Prager, in his book *Happiness Is a Serious Problem,* said that "happiness can be attained under virtually any circumstances providing you believe that your life has meaning and purpose."[96] Dan Baker and Cameron Stauth, in their book *What Happy People Know,* said that "happy people know why they're here on earth. They're doing the things they were meant to do. If they died today, they would be satisfied with their lives."[97]

Tal Ben-Shahar taught a popular course at Harvard on positive psychology. In his book *Happier,* he wrote that happiness is "the overall experience of pleasure and meaning."[98] Meaning comes from having a sense of purpose. He said:

> A happy person enjoys positive emotions while perceiving her life as purposeful. The definition does not pertain to a single moment but to a generalized aggregate of one's experiences: a person can endure emotional pain at times and still be happy overall.
>
> .... To live a meaningful life, we must have a self-generated purpose that possesses personal significance rather than one that is dictated by society's standards and expectations. When we do experience this sense of purpose, we often feel as though we have found our calling. As George Bernard Shaw said, 'This is the true joy of life, the being used for a purpose recognized by yourself as a mighty one.'[99]

By focusing on meaning, servant-leaders are intrinsically motivated, are psychologically healthier, and can find deep happiness.

Important Sources of Personal Meaning

There are at least four universal sources of personal meaning. These are four sources that are so fundamental that they cut across countries, cultures, and centuries. They can be found in most of the world's great religions and the teachings of many spiritual leaders. The four things you can do to find meaning are: Love people, help people, live ethically, and don't be too attached to material things.

I think there is a causal link between these four principles. If you love people, you will want to help them, and if you are loving and helping people, you will want to treat them right—you will want to treat them ethically. And if you are busy loving and helping others and treating them right, you are probably more focused on people than on things, so you probably aren't too attached to material things.

If I had to narrow it down even further, I would pick two core sources of meaning: (1) focus on others, and (2) become part of something larger than yourself. Focusing on others includes loving people, helping people, and treating them right. Becoming part of something larger than yourself is about joining with others in a team, an organization, a movement, a cause, a religion that makes a difference bigger than any of us can make as individuals. These sources of meaning are available to servant-leaders, every day.

"Symbols of Success" Are Not Enough

In our culture, leaders are rarely measured by how well they love people, help people, live ethically, and are not too attached to material things. Instead, they are usually measured by "symbols of success" like power, wealth, and fame.

What servant-leaders know is that the search for success and the search for meaning are not the same thing. They may overlap, but they are not the same. The things that our commercial, secular society considers to be attributes of success may have little to do with personal meaning.

For example, power is a symbol of success. But people learn that there is more meaning in helping people than in ordering them around. Wealth is a big symbol of success. But even the wealthy discover that there is more meaning in appreciating the richness of daily life—family, friends, hobbies, sunsets. Fame is a symbol of success, but the famous know that there is more meaning in being intimately known to a few people than being superficially known to millions of people. Winning is a symbol of success, but people learn that there is more meaning in always doing their personal best, win or lose.

The symbols of success are not necessarily bad. They're just *not enough.* It is not enough to get ahead. We also need to get meaning. This point was made dramatically by Edwin Arlington Robinson in his poem "Richard Cory."

Whenever Richard Cory went down town,
    We people on the pavement looked at him:
He was a gentleman from sole to crown,
    Clean favored, and imperially slim.

And he was always quietly arrayed,
    And he was always human when he talked;
But still he fluttered pulses when he said,
    "Good morning," and he glittered when he walked.

And he was rich—yes, richer than a king,
    And admirably schooled in every grace:
In fine, we thought that he was everything
    To make us wish that we were in his place.

So on we worked, and waited for the light,
    And went without the meat, and cursed the bread;
And Richard Cory, one calm summer night,
    Went home and put a bullet through his head.

We need more meaning in our lives than the "symbols of success" can provide. That is what I finally came to understand about Albert Schweitzer. He has been one of my heroes since I was a boy. Albert Schweitzer was one of the most brilliant and accomplished Europeans of his day. Born in 1875 in Alsace, Schweitzer distinguished himself early as an outstanding musician, philosopher, and theologian. Then, at age thirty, he began to study medicine and surgery to prepare for what he called "the direct service of humanity." In 1913, when he was thirty-eight, he and his wife left their comfortable lives in Europe and sailed to Western Africa, where they set up a crude hospital.

In their first year, the Schweitzers and their aides served over two thousand patients suffering from such diseases as malaria, yellow fever, and leprosy. Over the years, Schweitzer traveled to Europe and America to lecture and raise money for the hospital. He continued to serve others and promote his concept of reverence for life until his death in 1965.

I am impressed that Schweitzer gave up "success" for service. But I now realize that he gained more than he gave up.

Some people say that servant leadership is about giving up one's self-interest. They think a life of servant leadership is about self-sacrifice or self-denial. I disagree. *Servant leadership is not about self-sacrifice or self-denial. It is about self-fulfillment.* It is about living closely to your most important

66

sources of meaning, and thereby finding more meaning and deep happiness than are available in any other way.

Each of us has talents and abilities, and we should use them to the fullest. There is no point in going out into the world each day to fail. Servant-leaders work hard, and when they do, they are often "successful." But servant-leaders know that the symbols of success do not give them the deep happiness that comes from the most important sources of meaning in their lives and work.

Being Counter-Cultural

Of course, staying focused on the important sources of meaning in life can be "counter-cultural." TV and radio programs, movies, magazines and newspapers all promote the symbols of success. People who don't have these symbols of success are judged to be failures.

Robert Greenleaf knew that "to the worldly, servant-leaders may seem naïve .... [S]ervant-leaders may stand alone, largely without the support of their culture, as a saving remnant of those who care for both persons and institutions, and who are determined to make their caring count—*wherever they are involved.*"[100]

What our culture does not understand is that a "worldly" leader who seeks power, wealth, and fame, is not likely to be relevant or effective, and therefore, is not likely to be good for society. The "successful" leader will be focused on accumulating power, wealth, and fame, instead of identifying and meeting the needs of others. The symbols of success are a distraction that shifts the focus away from the needs of the organization and society at large. Thus, a "successful" leader may be a failure in terms of solving problems and seizing opportunities that will make the world a better place.

The most effective leaders do not seek power, wealth, or fame—they seek to make a difference in the lives of others. Paradoxically, when they *do* make a difference in the lives of others, they are often *given* power, wealth and fame. However, when that happens, they treat their power, wealth, and fame as tools to be used in helping others.

Personally Committed, Spiritually Liberated

One reason that people live a life of servant leadership is that it allows them to be personally committed and spiritually liberated. They make strong personal commitments to the mission and goals of their organizations. They bring their spirit and soul with them to fulfill those commitments. However, they are spiritually free. They love people and work hard to help them. But their organizations don't "own" them.

If servant-leaders were focused on the symbols of success that the organization can give or deny them, they might be at the mercy of the organization. But they are not focused on the symbols of success, so they are free from the coercive impact of those extrinsic motivators.

A servant-leader seeks opportunities to use his or her talents in service to others. Organizations are a great place to do that. Almost nothing in today's world is accomplished alone. We achieve more by working in teams.

However, a servant-leader is not afraid to leave an organization and seek a new way to serve, or even a new life, somewhere else. The paradox is that *this freedom to leave the organization gives dignity and meaning to the servant-leader's decision to stay.* When you know that you can leave and start a new life elsewhere, you go to work each day to freely give your time and talent. You aren't there because you are trapped and have to "do your time" until you retire. You are there to give the gifts you can give to help your organization succeed in serving others.

Work gives each employee a label, income, and status. It gives each employee a set of colleagues and the opportunity to make a difference in the world. But if your job is all that defines you, you may suffocate. You may do and say only those things that your boss or your organization wants you to do and say, because you can't imagine losing your job. Each day you go along, keep your head down, give in, and try to survive, even though something inside you is dying. You are fearful, clinging to the only job you know, afraid that you might lose it, and suffering a deep sadness because you do not have the courage to change your circumstances.

This is critically important. If your job is all that defines you, you will be tempted to "sell out" when a moral conflict arises, or you will be tempted to cling to your job even when your spiritual life is dying. Obviously, you will not be your best—you will not lead others with enthusiasm and confidence—if you are selling out or your spirit is dying.

In secular terms, spirit can be defined as "an attitude or principle that inspires, animates, or pervades thought, feeling, or action." You need to do things that inspire and animate you. You also need to bring your soul to work. In everyday language, soul can be defined as "the spiritual part of humans regarded in its moral aspect." You can't afford to lose your soul.

How do you achieve the freedom to leave for another position or start a new life? You achieve it by being bigger than your job—by defining yourself more broadly than the work you do for your organization. You define yourself in terms of your family, your friends, your faith, your values, your skills, your hobbies, your passions, your dreams. Your work gives you the opportunity to give of yourself, but your work is not your self. You are more than your job.

Knowing that you can find another leadership position, or even a new life elsewhere, gives you the freedom to be honest and authentic with others. You can speak the truth, and do what needs to be done, even when it puts your job at risk. You know that the worst thing is not losing your job. The worst thing is losing your spirit and your soul.

In his book *The Heart Aroused*, David Whyte tells the story of a friend who was in a meeting in which the CEO of his company asked the senior executives for their opinion of a plan that the CEO wanted to implement. He asked them to rate his plan on a scale of one to ten. It was clear that he was tired of people resisting his ideas. He wanted everyone in the room to give the plan a ten.

Whyte's friend knew that the plan was terrible, and everyone in the company would lose by it. He also knew that half the executives in the room understood that it was a bad plan. But as the CEO went around the room, calling on each executive, most of them gave the plan a ten. One gave it a nine and a half. Whyte's friend was the last to speak. Whyte says: "He reaches his hand toward the flame, opens his palm against the heat, and suddenly falters; against everything he believes, he hears a mouselike, faraway voice, his own, saying '*ten*.'"[101]

If he had said *zero*, he would have risked dismissal, or perhaps a slow lingering "death" on the sidelines of his organization. Whyte says that his friend said "ten" because he was not ready for a life somewhere else. He was afraid. And so he did something that diminished his spirit.

Perhaps he could have been more clever. Perhaps he could have given the CEO constructive suggestions about how to improve the plan to make it a "ten." But it might not have made a difference. The CEO wanted obedience, not honesty. He wanted "tens," not new ideas. Whyte's friend still might have ended up looking for another job, or languishing in the one he had.

These situations are never easy. But servant-leaders know they cannot do and be their best when their spirit and soul are being strangled. They are committed to service, so when the situation does not allow them to fulfill that commitment, they seek to serve elsewhere.

To thrive as a servant-leader, you don't need symbols of success. You need to get material results for your organization, but you need spiritual returns for yourself. You need the personal meaning that will feed your spirit and your soul and give you deep happiness. You need the kind of happiness that cannot come from power, wealth, or fame. You need the happiness that can only come from a life of service.

Postscript

And so I return to the point at which I began: There does not have to be so much pain and suffering, so much war and violence, so much starvation and disease, so many crushed dreams and untapped talents, so many problems unsolved and so many opportunities ignored. *The world does not have to be like this.*

Greenleaf said: "Servant-leaders differ from other persons of goodwill because they act on what they believe. Consequently, they 'know experimentally' and there is a sustaining spirit when they venture and risk."[102] With that sustaining spirit, servant-leaders can change the world. Many have already changed it; more are changing it today.

Changing the world for the better has never been easy. It not only takes hard work, it takes a dream. Greenleaf said:

> For anything to happen there must be a dream. And for anything great to happen there must be a great dream .... One of these great dreams is for the good society made up of predominantly serving institutions that shape its character by encouraging serving individuals and providing scope and shelter for large creative acts of service—by individuals and groups.[103]

Our dreams can reshape our world. Not all dreams come true; and if our dreams are big enough, they will not come true in our lifetimes. But we can still find meaning and deep happiness working toward our dreams.

Over the past thirty years, I have come to understand that *service is not just something you do. It's what life is about.* Nothing is more important, or more meaningful and fulfilling, than loving and helping others.

Albert Schweitzer said: "I don't know what your destiny will be, but one thing I know: the only ones among you who will be really happy are those who will have sought and found how to serve."

I wish you that happiness!

Questions for Reflection and Discussion

Chapter 1: It Starts With the Desire to Serve

1. Do you agree that service is considered to be important by the world's great religions and thinkers? If so, why do you think this is true? If not, why not?

2. Robert Coles said that "all service is directly or indirectly ethical activity, a reply to a moral call within, one that answers a moral need in the world." Do you agree? If so, why? If not, why not?

3. How do you serve others in your family, your school, your organization, or your community?

4. How does service to others give you "satisfactions"?

5. What is your opinion of people who devote a significant part of their lives to serving others?

6. What are three specific ways you can expand your service to others? Start one this week.

7. How can you remain focused on the needs of others?

Chapter 2: Who is a Servant-Leader?

1. How would you define a servant-leader? Write your own definition.

2. Name servant-leaders you know from history, literature, or real life today. What is it that makes them servant-leaders?

3. Name some famous leaders who were not servant-leaders. Why weren't they?

4. Read *Profiles in Courage* by John F. Kennedy. Which of the Senators in the book were servant-leaders? Explain.

5. In defining the servant-leader, Greenleaf said that the best test is: "Do those served grow as persons? Do they, *while being served*, become healthier, wiser, freer, more autonomous, more likely themselves to become servants? And, what is the effect on the least privileged in society? Will they benefit or at least not be further deprived?" Are there times when you have met this test? When and how?

Chapter 3: Power Model vs. Service Model

1. How would you define the power model of leadership?

2. How would you define the service model of leadership?

3. Make two columns and head one "power model" and the other one "service model." In each column, list words that describe each model. Which words are the same for both columns, and which are different?

4. To what end does a power-oriented leader use power? To what end does a servant-leader use power?

5. Which model of leadership have you used *most often?* Why?

6. Greenleaf said that serving each other requires love. He noted that love is undefinable. "But it begins, I believe, with one absolute condition: unlimited liability!" What does "unlimited liability" mean to you?

7. How does love become real in serving others?

8. Do you agree that serving others requires community?

Chapter 4: The Key Practices of Servant-Leaders

1. Do you think servant leadership works in all sectors—public, private, non-profit, and academic? Why or why not?

2. Are there ways in which any organization, in any sector, can contribute toward building a better society through servant leadership?

3. What are the specific practices of servant leadership?

4. Which practices make the most sense to you? Which make the least sense?

5. Which practices do you think are the hardest? The easiest?

6. Why is listening an important practice of servant-leaders?

7. How do you interpret the statement that servant-leaders don't begin with the answer?

8. What are the advantages of changing the traditional pyramidal hierarchy?

9. What does it mean to work for those who work for you?

10. Have you ever worked for a "boss" who was "controlling"? If so, how did you feel about your work?

11. Have you ever worked with a leader who was your "coach"? If so, how did you feel about your work?

12. Do you agree that foresight is the "lead" that the leader has?

Chapter 5: The Meaningful Lives of Servant-Leaders

1. Why do you think people become servant-leaders?

2. Why do you think people remain servant-leaders?

3. What is most attractive about servant leadership to you?

4. What is least attractive about servant leadership to you?

5. Do you believe in doing what is right and good and true, *anyway?* If so, why? If not, why not?

6. Are you more intrinsically motivated, or more extrinsically motivated? How do you know?

7. Do you think servant leadership is about self-denial and self-sacrifice, or about self-fulfillment? Why?

8. Have you experienced deep happiness in your life? When, and why?

9. Do you think that servant leadership is counter-cultural? Why, or why not?

10. What role does courage play in remaining a servant-leader? What kind of courage?

Appendix: Servant Leadership Compared with Other Ideas

Robert Greenleaf published his classic essay, *The Servant as Leader,* in 1970. He revised and republished it in 1973. Since then, there have been many new ideas or theories about leadership. How do these ideas or theories compare, or overlap, with servant leadership?

The answer depends partly on how you define servant leadership and how you define the other ideas or theories. In recent years, scholars have become interested in developing a theory of servant leadership in order to test it and compare it with other leadership theories. Based on the views of a number of scholars, the elements that are most unique to servant leadership compared with other theories are:

(1) the moral component, not only in terms of the personal morality and integrity of the servant-leader, but also in terms of the way in which a servant-leader encourages enhanced moral reasoning among his or her followers, who can therefore test the moral basis of the servant-leader's visions and organizational goals;

(2) the focus on serving followers for their own good, not just the good of the organization, and forming long-term relationships with followers, encouraging their growth and development so that over time they may reach their fullest potential;

(3) concern with the success of all stakeholders, broadly defined—employees, customers, business partners, communities, and society as a whole—including those who are the least privileged; and

(4) self-reflection, as a counter to the leader's hubris.[104]

A detailed comparison of servant leadership with other theories was published by Dirk van Dierendonck in the *Journal of Management*. He established six characteristics of servant-leaders, and then used them in his comparison (see Table 1). The six characteristics are: (1) empowering and developing people; (2) humility; (3) authenticity; (4) interpersonal acceptance; (5) providing direction; and (6) stewardship. Van Dierendonck compared these characteristics with the characteristics of seven leadership theories that he believed revealed the most overlap with servant leadership. Those theories were transformational leadership, authentic leadership, ethical leadership, Level 5 leadership, empowering leadership, spiritual leadership, and self-sacrificing leadership.

In comparing servant leadership with transformational leadership, van Dierendonck pointed out that servant leadership focuses on humility, authenticity, and interpersonal acceptance, none of which are explicit in transformational leadership. More specifically, transformational leaders focus on organizational objectives, while servant leaders focus more on concern for their followers. Van Dierendonck believes that authentic leadership could be incorporated into servant leadership, because it overlaps with servant leadership on two characteristics, authenticity and humility. However, servant leaders work for all stakeholders, whereas authentic leaders might focus on a single stakeholder, like shareholders.

Three servant leadership characteristics overlap with ethical leadership—empowering and developing people, humility, and stewardship. However, the other three characteristics of servant leadership—authenticity, interpersonal acceptance, and providing direction—are relatively unimportant in ethical leadership. Servant leadership overlaps with Level 5 leadership in humility and providing direction. However, elements like authenticity, interpersonal acceptance, and stewardship are clearly missing from the definition of Level 5 leadership.

The first characteristic of servant leadership, empowering and developing people, obviously overlaps with empowering leadership. However, empowering leadership does not include any of the other five characteristics of servant leadership. Van Dierendonck notes that it is unclear what behavior follows from spiritual leadership, so it is not clear how servant leadership and spiritual leadership might overlap. As for self-sacrificing leadership, he said that it is rooted in transformational

Table 1

Dr. Dirk van Dierendonck's comparison of his six characteristics of servant leadership with the characteristics of other leadership theories

	Six characteristics of servant leadership					
Leadership theories	Empowering	Humility	Authenticity	Interpersonal Acceptance	Providing Direction	Stewardship
Servant leadership	yes	yes	yes	yes	yes	yes
Transformational	yes	yes	yes		yes	yes
Authentic		yes	yes			
Ethical	yes	yes				
Level 5		yes				yes
Empowering*	yes				yes	
Spiritual*						
Self-sacrificing**	[yes]				[yes]	[yes]

*Behaviors of spiritual leadership are unknown, so it is not known how it would overlap

**Based on transformational leadership, and therefore presented in brackets

Van Dierendonck concluded that none of the seven theories incorporates all six characteristics of servant leadership, which puts servant leadership in a unique position. Additionally, servant leadership theory distinctly specifies a combined motivation to be(come) a leader with a need to serve that is at the foundation of these behaviors, and it is most explicit in emphasizing the importance of follower outcomes in terms of personal growth without necessarily being related to organizational outcomes.

From Dirk van Dierendonck, "Servant Leadership: A Review and Synthesis," *Journal of Management*, 2010. Table courtesy of Courtney Knies.

leadership, and different from servant leadership in its focus on the organization instead of the followers.

Van Dierendonck concluded that none of the seven theories incorporates all six of the characteristics of servant leadership, which puts servant leadership in a unique position. Additionally, servant leadership theory distinctly specifies a combined motivation to be(come) a leader with a need to serve that is at the foundation of these behaviors, and it is most explicit in emphasizing the importance of follower outcomes in terms of personal growth without necessarily being related to organizational outcomes.

Many people see the similarities between servant leadership and transforming leadership, as originally defined by James MacGregor Burns in his Pulitzer-Prize winning book, *Leadership.* Burns identified two basic types of leadership—transactional and transforming. He said:

> The relations of most leaders and followers are *transactional*— leaders approach followers with an eye to exchanging one thing for another: jobs for votes, or subsidies for campaign contributions. Such transactions comprise the bulk of the relationships among leaders and followers, especially in groups, legislatures, and parties. *Transforming* leadership, while more complex, is more potent. The transforming leader recognizes and exploits an existing need or demand of a potential follower. But, beyond that, the transforming leader looks for potential motives in followers, seeks to satisfy higher needs, and engages the full person of the follower. The result of transforming leadership is a relationship of mutual stimulation and elevation that converts followers into leaders and may convert leaders into moral agents.[105]

Burns suggested that the best modern example of a transforming leader was Gandhi, "who aroused and elevated the hopes and demands of millions of Indians and whose life and personality were enhanced in the process."[106]

Bernard Bass replaced the "transforming leader" described by Burns with the "transformational leader" mentioned above. A transformational leader inspires followers with a compelling mission and a vision, attends to their needs, and acts as a mentor or coach, drawing out their intrinsic motivation. A transformational leader encourages creativity and independent thinking, challenges the status quo, and serves as a role model of ethical behavior.

Jill W. Graham, in an article in *Leadership Quarterly*, and Mark Ehrhart, in an article in *Personnel Psychology*, compared servant leadership and transformational leadership. They argued that servant leadership defines stakeholders more broadly, even including the least privileged; encourages followers to enhance their moral reasoning capacities, so they can test the morality of the leader's visions and objectives; and serves followers for their own good as well as the good of the organization. As noted above, Van Dierendonck found that a transformational leader did not have the characteristics of humility, authenticity, and interpersonal acceptance that were included in his definition of servant leadership.

Many people see similarities between servant leadership and the Level 5 leaders described by Jim Collins in his book *Good to Great.* Level 5 is the highest level in his hierarchy of executive capabilities. Collins said:

> Level 5 leaders channel their ego needs away from themselves and into the larger goal of building a great company. It is not that Level 5 leaders have no ego or self-interest. Indeed, they are incredibly ambitious—but their ambition is first and foremost for the institution, not themselves.[107]

In his research, Collins found that the most effective leaders were both modest and willful, both humble and fearless. In interviews, the Level 5 leaders didn't talk about themselves, they talked about their companies and the contributions of other executives. Collins said that "the good-to-great leaders never wanted to become larger-than-life heroes. They never aspired to be put on a pedestal or become unreachable icons. They were seemingly ordinary people quietly producing extraordinary results."[108] While being modest, Level 5 leaders had "ferocious resolve, an almost stoic determination to do whatever needs to be done to make the company great."[109]

It is reported that some of the researchers working with Collins suggested using the name "servant-leader" instead of Level 5 leader. Van Dierendonck argues that servant leadership and Level 5 leadership share the elements of humility and providing direction, but servant leadership elements like authenticity, interpersonal acceptance, and stewardship are not part of the definition of Level 5 leadership.

Servant leadership has elements in common with the ideas of stewardship and co-leadership. Peter Block, in his book *Stewardship*, proposed replacing the concept of leadership with the concept of stewardship. He said that stewardship is "the willingness to be accountable for the well-being of the larger organization by operating in service, rather than in control, of those around us."[110] Authentic service exists when there is a balance of power, the primary commitment is to the larger community, each person joins in defining purpose and deciding what kind of culture the organization will become, and there is a balanced and equitable distribution of rewards.

Stewardship involves partnership rather than patriarchy, and empowerment instead of dependency. This requires the deepening of one's commitment to service instead of self-interest. Block wrote:

> The antidote to self-interest is to commit and to find a cause ....
> Let the commitment and cause be the place where we work. It
> is not so much the product or service of our workplace that will
> draw us out of ourselves. It is the culture and texture and ways
> of creating community that attract our attention. Our task is to
> create organizations we believe in and to do it as an offering, not a
> demand.[110]

In their book *Co-Leaders: The Power of Great Partnerships*, David Heenan and Warren Bennis described the essential roles played by people who are not the stars or celebrities in their organizations, but rather key subordinates—deputies, chief operating officers, or vice presidents who are committed, skilled, supportive partners and members of the leadership team. "We know that every successful organization has, at its heart, a cadre of co-leaders—key players who do the work, even if they receive little of the glory."[112] They observed that in co-leadership:

> Power and responsibility are dispersed, giving the enterprise a
> whole constellation of costars—co-leaders with shared values and
> aspirations, all of whom work together toward common goals
> .... Successful costars are consummate team players and, thus,
> valuable models for everyone interested in effective collaboration.
> Usually servant-leaders, they tend to be self-reliant, yet committed
> to organizational goals .... Outstanding co-leaders know that they
> don't have to be at the top of the organizational chart to find
> satisfaction— that exercising one's gifts and serving a worthy cause
> are far more reliable sources of satisfaction than the title on one's
> office door.[113]

It is important to remember that Greenleaf did not propose servant
leadership as an academic theory, but as a philosophy with a set of
practices. The importance of serving others is recognized throughout
the world. As Stephen Prosser noted in his essay, *Servant Leadership: More
Philosophy, Less Theory,* Greenleaf did not invent the concept of service.
However:

> ... [Greenleaf] articulated, as a new and appropriate voice within
> the twentieth century (and for the twenty-first century and beyond),
> a concept that has been the bedrock of civilized and compassionate
> existence for centuries. Greenleaf's major contribution has been to
> show that this principle, this philosophy of life in general, can exist
> and have credence within modern organizational life .... To treat
> servant leadership as if it were only another general leadership
> theory runs the risk of missing the full depth of Greenleaf's
> thinking, devaluing the philosophical, moral, spiritual, historical,
> cultural and intellectual fascination inherent in his work." (pp.40-
> 41)

Prosser concluded that if one needed to create a theory to explain
Greenleaf's writings, it would not be a theory of leadership, it would be a
theory of servanthood.

Sources

James A. Autry, *The Servant Leader: How to Build a Creative Team, Develop Great Morale, and Improve Bottom-Line Performance* (Roseville, California: Prima Publishing, 2001).

Dan Baker and Cameron Stauth, *What Happy People Know: How the New Science of Happiness Can Change Your Life for the Better* (Emmaus, Pennsylvania: Rodale, Inc., 2003).

Chester I. Barnard, *The Functions of the Executive* (Cambridge, Massachusetts: Harvard University Press, 1966).

Howard Behar, *It's Not About the Coffee: Leadership Principles from a Life at Starbucks* (New York: Penguin Group, 2007).

Tal Ben-Shahar, *Happier: Learn the Secrets to Daily Joy and Lasting Fulfillment* (New York: McGraw Hill, 2007).

Ken Blanchard, "Foreword: The Heart of Servant Leadership," in Larry C. Spears and Michele Lawrence, eds., *Focus on Leadership: Servant Leadership for the Twenty-First Century* (New York: John Wiley & Sons, Inc., 2002).

Ken Blanchard and the Founding Associates and Consulting Partners of the Ken Blanchard Companies, *Leading at a Higher Level: Blanchard on Leadership and Creating High Performing Organizations* (Upper Saddle River, New Jersey: Blanchard Management Corporation Publishing as Prentice Hall, 2007).

Ken Blanchard, Scott Blanchard, and Drea Zigarmi, Chapter 12, "Servant Leadership," in Ken Blanchard and the Founding Associates and Consulting Partners of the Ken Blanchard Companies, *Leading at a Higher Level: Blanchard on Leadership and Creating High Performing Organizations* (Upper Saddle River, New Jersey: Blanchard Management Corporation Publishing as Prentice Hall, 2007).

Peter Block, *Stewardship: Choosing Service Over Self-Interest* (San Francisco: Berrett-Koehler Publishers, 1993).

Juana Bordas, *Salsa, Soul, and Spirit: Leadership for a Multicultural Age* (San Francisco: Berrett-Koehler Publishers, Inc., 2007).

James MacGregor Burns, *Leadership* (New York: Harper & Row, Publishers, 1978).

Robert Coles, *The Call of Service* (Boston: Houghton Mifflin Company, 1993).

Jim Collins, *Good to Great: Why Some Companies Make the Leap ... and Others Don't* (New York: HarperCollinsPublishers, 2001).

Stephen Covey, "Foreword: Servant Leadership from the Inside Out," in Larry C. Spears, ed., *Insights on Leadership: Service, Stewardship, Spirit, and Servant Leadership* (New York: John Wiley & Sons, Inc., 1998).

Edward L. Deci, *Why We Do What We Do: Understanding Self-Motivation* (New York: G. P. Putnam's Sons, 1995).

Max De Pree, *Leadership Is an Art* (New York: Doubleday, 1989).

Peter F. Drucker, *The Effective Executive* (New York: Harper & Row, Publishers, 1967).

Eknath Easwaran, trans., *The Bhagavad Gita* (Tomales, California: Nilgiri Press, 1985).

Dan R. Ebener, *The Servant Parish: A Case Study of Servant Leadership and Organizational Citizenship Behaviors in High-Performing Catholic Parishes* (Dissertation presented to the Doctoral Faculty Council of St. Ambrose University in partial fulfillment of the requirements for the degree Doctor of Business Administration, May 2007.) See also, Dan Ebener, *Servant Leadership Models for Your Parish* (New York: Paulist Press, 2010).

Mark G. Ehrhart, "Leadership and Procedural Justice Climate as Antecedents of Unit-Level Organizational Citizenship Behavior, *Personnel Psychology*, 57, 61-94 (2004).

Joseph J. Ellis, *Founding Brothers: The Revolutionary Generation* (New York: Vintage Books, 2000).

Ezekiel, in *The Holy Bible*, New International Version (Grand Rapids, Michigan: Zondervan Bible Publishers, 1978).

Don M. Frick, *Greenleaf and Servant-Leader Listening* (Westfield, Indiana: The Greenleaf Center for Servant Leadership, 2011).

Viktor E. Frankl, *Man's Search for Meaning: An Introduction to Logotherapy* (New York: Pocket Books, 1963).

Daniel Goleman, Richard Boyatzis, and Annie McKee, *Primal Leadership: Learning to Lead with Emotional Intelligence* (Boston, Massachusetts: Harvard Business School Press, 2002).

Jill W. Graham, "Servant Leadership in Organizations: Inspirational and Moral," *Leadership Quarterly*, 2 (2), 105-119 (1991).

Robert Greene, *The 48 Laws of Power* (New York: Penguin Putnam Inc., 1998).

Robert K. Greenleaf, *Servant Leadership: A Journey into the Nature of Legitimate Power and Greatness* (New York: Paulist Press, 1977).

Robert K. Greenleaf, *The Institution as Servant* (Westfield, Indiana: The Greenleaf Center for Servant Leadership, 1972/2009).

Robert K. Greenleaf, *"The Leadership Crisis,"* in Larry Spears, ed., *The Power of Servant Leadership* (San Francisco: Berrett-Koehler Publishers, Inc., 1998).

Robert K. Greenleaf, *The Servant as Leader* (Westfield, Indiana: The Greenleaf Center for Servant Leadership, 1970/2008).

Robert K. Greenleaf, *Trustees as Servants* (Westfield, Indiana: The Greenleaf Center for Servant Leadership, 1974/2009).

John Hagell III, John Seely Brown, and Lang Davison, *The Power of Pull: How Small Moves, Smartly Made, Can Set Big Things in Motion* (New York: Basic Books, 2010).

David A. Heenan and Warren Bennis, *Co-Leaders: The Power of Great Partnerships* (New York: John Wiley & Sons, Inc., 1999).

John Heider, *The Tao of Leadership: Lao Tzu's* Tao Te Ching *Adapted for a New Age* (New York: Bantam Books, 1986).

Joseph Jaworski, *Synchronicity: The Inner Path of Leadership* (San Francisco: Berrett-Koehler Publishers, 1996).

Gospel of John (13:12-15), in *The Holy Bible, New International Version*, 1431-1432.

Kent M. Keith, *Do It Anyway: The Handbook for Finding Personal Meaning and Deep Happiness in a Crazy World* (Makawao, Maui, Hawaii: Inner Ocean Publishing, Inc., 2003).

Kent M. Keith, *Morality and Morale: A Business Tale* (Honolulu: Terrace Press, 2012).

Kent M. Keith, *The Silent Revolution: Dynamic Leadership in the Student Council* (Cambridge, Massachusetts: Harvard Student Agencies, Inc., 1968).

Daniel Kim, *Foresight as the Central Ethic of Leadership* (Westfield, Indiana: The Greenleaf Center for Servant Leadership, 2002).

James M. Kouzes and Barry Z. Posner, *A Leader's Legacy* (San Francisco: Jossey-Bass, 2006).

James M. Kouzes and Barry Z. Posner, *The Leadership Challenge* (Fourth Edition) (San Francisco: Jossey-Bass, 2007).

Richard Layard, *Happiness: Lessons from a New Science* (New York: The Penguin Press, 2005).

C. S. Lewis, *The Abolition of Man* (New York: The Macmillan Company, 1947).

Lao Tzu, *Tao Teh Ching*, trans. John C. H. Wu (Boston, Massachusetts: Shambhala, 2006).

Max Lerner, Introduction, *The Prince and The Discourses by Niccolo Machiavelli* (New York: The Modern Library, 1950).

Robert C. Liden, Sandy J. Wayne, Hao Zhao and David Henderson, "Servant Leadership: Development of a Multidimensional Measure and Multi-level Assessment," *The Leadership Quarterly*, 19, 161-177 (2008).

Isabel Lopez, "Finding Wisdom and Purpose in Chaotic Times," in Robert Banks and Kimberly Powell, eds., *Faith in Leadership* (San Francisco: Jossey-Bass, 2000).

Niccolo Machiavelli, *The Prince and the Discourses* (New York: The Modern Library, 1950).

Gospel of Matthew (20:25-28), in *The Holy Bible, New International Version* (Grand Rapids, Michigan: Zondervan Bible Publishers, 1978).

Ann McGee-Cooper and Gary Looper, *The Essentials of Servant Leadership: Principles in Practice* (Waltham, Massachusetts: Pegasus Communications, Inc., 2001).

Ann McGee-Cooper, Gary Looper, and Duane Trammell, *Being the Change: Profiles from Our Servant Leadership Learning Community* (Dallas, Texas: Ann McGee-Cooper and Associates, 2007).

Douglas McGregor, *The Human Side of Enterprise* (New York: McGraw-Hill, 1960/2006).

Ken Melrose, *Making the Grass Greener on Your Side: A CEO's Journey to Leading by Serving* (San Francisco: Berrett-Koehler Publishers, 1995).

Pastoral Institute, Columbus, Georgia, website: www.pilink.org

Dennis Prager, *Happiness Is a Serious Problem: A Human Nature Repair Manual* (New York: Regan Books, 1998).

Stephen Prosser, *Servant Leadership: More Philosophy, Less Theory* (Westfield, Indiana: The Greenleaf Center for Servant Leadership, 2010).

Steven B. Sample, *The Contrarian's Guide to Leadership* (San Francisco: Jossey-Bass, 2002).

Yasin Khalaf Sarayrah, "Servant leadership in the Bedouin-Arab culture," *Global Virtue Ethics Review*, Volume Five, Number 3, 58-79 (2004).

Peter M. Senge, "Robert Greenleaf's Legacy: A New Foundation for Twenty-First Century Institutions," in Larry C. Spears, ed., *Reflections on Leadership: How Robert K. Greenleaf's Theory of Servant Leadership Influenced Today's Top Management Thinkers* (New York: John Wiley & Sons, Inc. 1995).

James D. Showkeir, "The Business Case for Servant Leadership," in Larry C. Spears and Michele Lawrence, eds., *Focus on Leadership: Servant Leadership for the Twenty-First Century* (New York: John Wiley & Sons, Inc., 2002).

Larry C. Spears and Michele Lawrence, eds., *Focus on Leadership: Servant Leadership for the Twenty-First Century* (New York: John Wiley & Sons, Inc., 2002).

Larry Spears, ed., *Reflections on Leadership: How Robert K. Greenleaf's Theory of Servant Leadership Influenced Today's Top Management Thinkers* (New York: John Wiley & Sons, Inc. 1995).

Kenneth W. Thomas, *Intrinsic Motivation at Work: Building Energy and Commitment* (San Francisco: Berrett-Koehler Publishers, Inc., 2002).

Noel M. Tichy and Warren G. Bennis, *Judgment: How Winning Leaders Make Great Calls* (New York: The Penguin Group, 2007).

William B. Turner, *The Learning of Love: A Journey Toward Servant Leadership* (Macon, Georgia: Smyth & Helwys, 2000).

Dirk van Dierendonck, "Servant Leadership: A Review and Synthesis," *Journal of Management*, published online by Sage, 2 September 2010, at http://jom.sagepub.com/content/early/2010/09/01/0149206310380462.

Fred O. Walumbwa, Chad A. Hartnell and Adegoke Oke, "Servant Leadership, Procedural Justice Climate, Service Climate, Employee Attitudes, and Organizational Citizenship Behavior: A Cross-Level Investigation," *Journal of Applied Psychology*, Vol. 95, No. 3, 517-529 (2010).

Margaret J. Wheatley, *Leadership and the New Science* (San Francisco: Berrett-Koehler Publishers, Inc., 1994).

Margaret Wheatley, "The Work of the Servant-Leader," in Larry C. Spears and Michele Lawrence, eds., *Focus on Leadership: Servant Leadership for the Twenty-First Century* (New York: John Wiley & Sons, Inc., 2002).

David Whyte, *The Heart Aroused: Poetry and the Preservation of the Soul in Corporate America* (New York: Doubleday, 1994).

Andrew Wilson, ed., *World Scripture: A Comparative Anthology of Sacred Texts* (St. Paul, Minnesota: Paragon House, 1995).

Muhammad Yunus, *Creating a World Without Poverty* (New York: Public Affairs, 2007).

Notes

[1] Greenleaf, *Servant Leadership*, 13.

[2] Coles, *The Call of Service*, 69-70.

[3] Easwaran, *The Bhagavad Gita*, 76.

[4] Many of the quotations in this section are from Chapter 19, "Live for Others," in Wilson, *World Scripture*, 683-690.

[5] Lewis, *The Abolition of Man*, 115-116.

[6] Coles, *The Call of Service*, 75.

[7] Lao Tzu, *Tao Teh Ching*, 35.

[8] Heider, *The Tao of Leadership*, 33.

[9] Ezekiel (34: 2-10), in *The Holy Bible, New International Version*, 1153. The hadith of the Prophet Muhammed is quoted by Yasin Khalaf Sarayrah, in "Servant leadership in the Bedouin-Arab culture," *Global Virtue Ethics Review*, 75.

[10] Gospel of Matthew (20:25-28), in *The Holy Bible, New International Version*, 1318. See also Mark 10:42-45, page 1350.

[11] Gospel of John (13:12-15), in *The Holy Bible, New International Version*, 1431-1432.

[12] Greenleaf, *The Servant as Leader*, 15.

[13] Greenleaf, *The Institution as Servant*, 9.

[14] Spears, *Reflections on Leadership*, 4-7.

[15] Website of the Pastoral Institute, Columbus, Georgia: www.pilink.org.

[16] Liden, Wayne, Zhao, and Henderson, "Servant leadership: Development of a multidimensional measure and multi-level assessment," *The Leadership Quarterly*.

[17] Dirk van Dierendonck, "Servant Leadership: A Review and Synthesis," *Journal of Management*.

[18] Keith, *Do It Anyway*, 89.

[19] Tichy and Bennis, *Judgment*, 67-69.

[20] Greenleaf, *The Servant as Leader*, 9.

[21] The phrases "power model of leadership" and "service model of leadership" are mine, not Greenleaf's. They do not refer to theoretical models, but to a set of ideas or as-

sumptions that focus on leadership as an expression of personal power, on the one hand, and leadership as an opportunity for service, on the other hand. For example, Theory X would fit under the power model, while Theory Y and servant leadership would fit under the service model; "push" would fit under the power model, while "pull" would fit under the service model. See Douglas McGregor, *The Human Side of Enterprise*, and John Hagel III, John Seely Brown, and Lang Davison, *The Power of Pull*.

[22] Greenleaf, *The Servant as Leader*, 44.

[23] Lerner, Introduction, *The Prince* , xxx.

[24] Machiavelli, *The Prince*, 35.

[25] Id., 56.

[26] Id., 64.

[27] Id., 79.

[28] Greene, *The 48 Laws of Power*, xvii.

[29] Greenleaf, *The Institution as Servant*, 9.

[30] Ellis, *Founding Brothers*, 130.

[31] Autry, *The Servant Leader*, 21.

[32] Greenleaf, *The Servant as Leader*, 11-12.

[33] Greenleaf, "The Leadership Crisis," 87–88.

[34] Greenleaf, *The Servant as Leader*, 39.

[35] Id., 39-40.

[36] Turner, *The Learning of Love*, 158.

[37] Bordas, *Salsa, Soul, and Spirit*, 119.

[38] Id., 120.

[39] Id., 121.

[40] Wheatley, *The Work of the Servant-Leader*, 360-361.

[41] Blanchard, "Foreword: The Heart of Servant Leadership," xi.

[42] Blanchard, *Leading at a Higher Level*, 269.

[43] See Chapter 12, "Servant Leadership," by Ken Blanchard, Scott Blanchard, and Drea Zigarmi, in *Leading at a Higher Level*, 249-276.

[44] Covey, "Foreword: Servant Leadership from the Inside Out," xi-xii.

[45] Drucker, *The Effective Executive*, 52-53.

[46] Senge, "Robert Greenleaf's Legacy: A New Foundation for Twenty-First Century Institutions," 217-218.

[47] For the impacts of servant leadership in the workplace, the following articles are available: Mark G. Ehrhart, "Leadership and procedural justice climate as antecedents of unit-level organizational citizenship behavior, *Personnel Psychology*, 57, 61-94 (2004); Robert C. Liden, Sandy J. Wayne, Hao Zhao, and David Henderson, "Servant leadership: Development of a multidimensional measure and multilevel assessment," *Leadership Quarterly*, 19, 161-177 (2008); D. M. Mayer, M. Bardes, and R. F. Piccolo, " Do servant-leaders help satisfy follower needs? An organizational justice perspective," *European Journal of Work and Organizational Psychology*, 17, 180-197 (2008); M. J. Neubert, K.M. Kacmar, D. S. Carlson, L. B. Chonko, & J.A. Roberts, "Regulatory focus as a mediator of the influence of initiating structure and servant leadership on employee behavior, *Journal of Applied Psychology*, 93(6), 1220-1233 (2008); R. F. Piccolo and J. A. Colquitt, "Transformational leadership and job behaviors: The mediating role of core job characteristics," *Academy of Management Journal*, 49, 327-340 (2006); and Fred O. Walumbwa, Chad A. Hartnell, & Adegoke Oke, "Servant leadership, procedural justice climate, service climate, employee attitudes, and organizational citizenship behavior: A cross-level investigation, *Journal of Applied Psychology*, 95, 517-529 (2010).

[48] Personal communication with Jack Lowe, Jr., August 20, 2007. The quote is a variation of a quote found in Ann McGee-Cooper and Gary Looper, *The Essentials of Servant Leadership: Principles in Practice*, 9.

[49] Kouzes and Posner, *A Leader's Legacy*, 64.

[50] Goleman, Boyatzis, and McKee, *Primal Leadership*, 8-9.

[51] Lopez, "Finding Wisdom and Purpose in Chaotic Times," 85-86.

[52] Greenleaf, *The Servant as Leader*, 18. See also Don M. Frick, *Greenleaf and Servant-Leader Listening*.

[53] Id., 16.

[54] Yunus, *Creating a World Without Poverty*, 45–47.

[55] Greenleaf, *The Institution as Servant*, 23-24.

[56] Turner, *The Learning of Love*,151.

[57] Blanchard, *Leading at a Higher Level*, 250.

[58] Sample, *The Contrarian's Guide to Leadership*, 121.

[59] Id., 121-122.

[60] Autry, *The Servant Leader,* 20.

[61] Greenleaf, *The Servant as Leader,* 15.

[62] Greenleaf, *Servant Leadership,* 154–159.

[63] Drucker, *The Effective Executive,* 59.

[64] Id., 60.

[65] Showkeir, "The Business Case for Servant Leadership," 158.

[66] Id.

[67] Kouzes and Posner, *A Leader's Legacy,* 79.

[68] Autry, *The Servant Leader,* 20-21.

[69] Quoted in Ann McGee-Cooper and Gary Looper, *The Essentials of Servant Leadership: Principles in Practice,* 11.

[70] Barnard, *The Functions of the Executive,* 165.

[71] Personal communication with Jack Lowe, Jr., August 20, 2007.

[72] Wheatley, *Leadership and the New Science,* 38-39.

[73] Covey, "Foreword: Servant Leadership from the Inside Out," xi-xii.

[74] Ebener, *The Servant Parish.*

[75] Quoted in a TDIndustries brochure. Found also in McGee-Cooper, Looper, and Trammell, *Being the Change,* 14-15.

[76] Showkeir, "The Business Case for Servant Leadership," 160-161.

[77] Behar, *It's Not About the Coffee,* 55.

[78] Thomas, *Intrinsic Motivation at Work,* 44.

[79] Kouzes and Posner, *The Leadership Challenge,* 115.

[80] Melrose, *Making The Grass Greener On Your Side,* 6.

[81] Greenleaf, *The Servant as Leader,* 25.

[82] Id., 26.

[83] Id., 27.

[84] Kim, *Foresight as the Central Ethic of Leadership,* 3.

[85] Id.

[86] Collins, *Good to Great*, 65-69.

[87] Tichy and Bennis, *Judgment*, 157-159.

[88] Jaworski, *Synchronicity*, 182.

[89] De Pree, *Leadership Is an Art*, 14-15.

[90] Keith, *The Silent Revolution*, 11.

[91] Thomas, *Intrinsic Motivation at Work*, 46.

[92] Id., 22.

[93] Frankl, *Man's Search for Meaning*, 154.

[94] Deci, *Why We Do What We Do*, 128.

[95] Layard, *Happiness: Lessons from a New Science*, 22.

[96] Prager, *Happiness Is a Serious Problem*, 101.

[97] Baker and Stauth, *What Happy People Know*, 21.

[98] Ben-Shahar, *Happier: Learn the Secrets to Daily Joy and Lasting Fulfillment*, 33.

[99] Id., 33-39.

[100] Greenleaf, *Servant Leadership*, 329-330.

[101] Whyte, *The Heart Aroused*, 117-118.

[102] Greenleaf, *Servant Leadership*, 329.

[103] Id., 88.

[104] See, for example, Jill W. Graham, "Servant leadership in organizations: Inspirational and moral," *Leadership Quarterly*; Mark G. Ehrhart, "Leadership and procedural justice climate as antecedents of unit-level organizational citizenship behavior, *Personnel Psychology*; Robert C. Liden, Sandy J. Wayne, Hao Zhao, and David Henderson, "Servant leadership: Development of a multidimensional measure and multilevel assessment," *Leadership Quarterly*; Fred O. Walumbwa, Chad A. Hartnell, and Adegoke Oke, "Servant leadership, procedural justice climate, service climate, employee attitudes, and organizational citizenship behavior: A cross-level investigation, *Journal of Applied Psychology*.

[105] Burns, *Leadership*, 4.

[106] Id., 20.

[107] Collins, *Good to Great*, 21.

[108] Id., 28.

[109] Id., 30.

[110] Block, *Stewardship: Choosing Service Over Self-Interest*, xx.

[111] Id., 10.

[112] Heenan and Bennis, *Co-Leaders*, 3.

[113] Id., 5–12.

Acknowledgments

I would like to thank those who commented on the first edition of the book while it was being written: Dr. Carolyn Crippen, Charley Bellinger, Jerry Glashagel, Dr. Dan Ebener, Dr. Stuart Gothold, Rev. Dan Hatch, Dr. John Horsman, Gary Kent, Isabel Lopez, Geneva Loudd, Jack Lowe, Jr., Dr. Ann McGee-Cooper, Dr. Fran Newman, Richard Pieper, Kay Stone, Christine Van Meter, Ed Voerman, Dr. Margit Watts, and my wife, Dr. Elizabeth Keith. My thanks to those who reviewed and commented on the second edition: Phil Anderson, Dolores Jones, Courtney Knies, Isabel Lopez, and Dr. Ann McGee-Cooper. I am grateful to them all for the gift of their time and insight.

About the Author

Dr. Kent M. Keith has been an attorney, state government official, high tech park developer, university president, YMCA executive, and full-time speaker and author. From 2007 to 2012 he served as the Chief Executive Officer of the Greenleaf Center for Servant Leadership in Indiana.

Dr. Keith earned a B.A. in Government from Harvard University, an M.A. in Philosophy and Politics from Oxford University in England, a Certificate in Japanese from Waseda University in Tokyo, a J.D. from the University of Hawaii, and an Ed. D. from the University of Southern California. He is a Rhodes Scholar.

Dr. Keith is known throughout the world as the author of the Paradoxical Commandments, which he first published in 1968 in a booklet for student leaders. During the past ten years he has published four books about the commandments, including *Anyway: The Paradoxical Commandments*, which became a national bestseller and was translated into 17 languages. He is also the author of three books on servant leadership: *The Case for Servant Leadership; Servant Leadership in the Boardroom: Fulfilling the Public Trust;* and *Questions and Answers about Servant Leadership*.

Over the years, Dr. Keith has given more than 1,000 presentations, conference papers, and seminars on a wide variety of topics in the United States and eight countries in Europe and Asia. His current presentations and seminars are focused on servant leadership, the Paradoxical Commandments, finding personal meaning at home and at work, and the positive impact of morality in the workplace. He has been featured on the front page of *The New York Times* and in *People* magazine, *The Washington Post*, *The San Francisco Chronicle*, and *Family Circle*. He was interviewed by Katie Couric on NBC's *Today Show* and by Dr. Robert H. Schuller on *The Hour of Power*. He has been quoted in *The Wall Street Journal* and *Inc.com*. He has appeared on dozens of TV shows and more than 100 radio programs in the United States, the United Kingdom, Japan, Korea, and Australia.

More information about Dr. Keith and his work is available at www.kentmkeith.com. He may be contacted at: drkentkeith@hotmail.com.

Other books by Dr. Kent M. Keith

Servant Leadership:

Questions and Answers about Servant Leadership
by Kent M. Keith
(Greenleaf Center for Servant Leadership, 2012)

During the past two decades, Dr. Keith has given hundreds of speeches and workshops on servant leadership. This book shares the questions that he is often asked and the answers that he gives when he is making presentations. In some cases, the answers have been expanded for this publication. This book will be especially useful to those who naturally begin with questions, whether they are new to servant leadership or have been on the journey for many years. The book provides the reader with starting points for further study, reflection, and implementation. Where applicable, answers conclude with recommendations for additional reading. A list of all the recommended readings can be found at the end of the text.
Available from www.toservefirst.com

Servant Leadership in the Boardroom: Fulfilling the Public Trust
by Kent M. Keith
(Greenleaf Center for Servant Leadership, 2011)

This book presents and augments the views of Robert Greenleaf on the opportunity of board members of all types of corporations—for-profit and non-profit—to truly lead and make a difference for their organizations and those their organizations serve. The book provides historical background on the public purpose of all corporations, the responsibilities of board members as trustees for the public good, the unique value of board judgments, the relationship between the board and administration, and keys to board effectiveness, including the board as a "council of equals" that focuses on what matters most, asking fundamental questions and seeking information about how well the organization is serving its employees and society at large.
Available from www.toservefirst.com

Morality and Morale: A Business Tale
by Kent M. Keith
(Terrace Press, 2012)

Morality and Morale: A Business Tale is a story about a young business manager faced with a moral dilemma at work. As he calls on others for advice, he learns that business is a way to serve others; that there is a universal moral code that each of us can follow in our businesses and our private lives; that morality and morale are related, so that when morality goes up, so does morale; that treating others right can be a source of personal energy and can result in business success; and that living morally makes life more meaningful. The book includes Notes for the Reader with background on the ideas introduced in the story. **Available from www.moralityandmorale.com**

Paradoxical Commandments:

Anyway: The Paradoxical Commandments
by Kent M. Keith
(G. P. Putnam's Sons, 2002).

The Paradoxical Commandments were first written by Kent Keith in 1968, when he was 19, as part of a booklet for student leaders. The commandments subsequently spread around the world, and have been used by millions of people. This book is an introduction to the Paradoxical Commandments and what they mean. It was a national bestseller in the United States, and has been translated into 17 languages.
Available from www.paradoxicalcommandments.com

Do It Anyway: Finding Personal Meaning and Deep Happiness by Living the Paradoxical Commandments
by Kent M. Keith
(Inner Ocean Publishing, 2003; New World Library, 2008).

This book is a companion to *Anyway: The Paradoxical Commandments*. It describes how people have used the Paradoxical Commandments to break away from their daily excuses, or a painful past, or a complicated present, to find meaning anyway. This is a practical "how to" book for those who want to put the Paradoxical Commandments into practice in their own lives. The book includes forty stories about people who are living the commandments; questions for personal reflection and group discussion; and an interview with the author in which he answers the questions he is asked most often about the commandments.
Available from www.paradoxicalcommandments.com

Jesus Did It Anyway: The Paradoxical Commandments for Christians
by Kent M. Keith
(G. P. Putnam's Sons, 2005).

For more than forty years, the Paradoxical Commandments have been used by Christians all over the globe. Mother Teresa thought they were important enough to put on the wall of her children's home in Calcutta. *Jesus Did It Anyway* illustrates the Paradoxical Commandments through stories and verses from both the Old Testament and the New Testament, the teachings of Jesus and the apostles, and personal anecdotes. The 14-chapter book includes a study guide with questions for each chapter.
Available from www.paradoxicalchristians.com

Have Faith Anyway: The Vision of Habakkuk for Our Times
by Kent M. Keith
(Jossey-Bass, 2008).

Have Faith Anyway explores the author's new eleventh Paradoxical Commandment: *The world is full of violence, injustice, starvation, disease, and environmental destruction. Have faith anyway.* To help the reader better understand what it is like to have faith in the face of seemingly insurmountable problems, the author tells the story of the Old Testament prophet Habakkuk, whose vision of a conversation with God led him to an inspiring affirmation of faith even in the face of devastation and death. The book concludes with the author's own vision of a conversation between a Christian and God today. The book includes a Readers Guide for Reflection and Study.
Available from www.paradoxicalchristians.com

ᵧh School Student Council Leadership:

The Silent Revolution: Dynamic Leadership in the Student Council
by Kent M. Keith
(Harvard Student Agencies, 1968; Terrace Press, 2003)

This is the book for which Dr. Keith wrote the Paradoxical Commandments, 149 words that have spread all over the world and have been used by millions of people of all ages and backgrounds. The book was first published in 1968, when Dr. Keith was 19, a sophomore in college. In the book, Keith encourages student leaders to work together, through the system, to achieve positive, lasting change. He believes that students councils can, and should, make a difference. He explains the need to love people, and do what is meaningful and satisfying, whether you get credit or not. He uses hypothetical stories to describe practical leadership skills and dilemmas, argues that the "good guys" can win, and urges students to take action now. "Don't vegetate," he says. "Initiate."
Available from www.paradoxicalcommandments.com

The Silent Majority: The Problem of Apathy and the Student Council
by Kent M. Keith
(National Association of Secondary School Principals, 1971; Terrace Press, 2004)

Dr. Keith was 20, a junior in college, when he wrote this book as a companion to his first book, *The Silent Revolution: Dynamic Leadership in the Student Council.* Keith says: *"The Silent Majority* is written from high school student council leaders who want to give the student council its noblest meaning and purpose: people helping people." Keith argues that no one is completely apathetic—everyone is interested in *something.* It's up to student leaders to find out what their fellow students are interested in, and then link up with those interests. In the process, student leaders will learn more about themselves, and discover the richness of life that is available to those who become "people people."
Available from www.paradoxicalcommandments.com

THE ART OF

Erotic

MASSAGE

THE ART OF

Erotic

MASSAGE

Dr ANDREW YORKE

BLANDFORD

First published in the UK 1988 by
Blandford Press
an imprint of Cassell plc,
Villiers House, 41–47 Strand,
London WC2N 5JE

Distributed in the United States by
Sterling Publishing Co., Inc.,
387 Park Avenue South, New York, NY 10016

Distributed in Australia by
Capricorn Link (Australia) Pty Ltd,
PO Box 665, Lane Cove, NSW 2066

Reprinted 1989 (twice), 1990, 1991

British Library Cataloguing in Publication Data

Yorke, Andrew.
  The art of erotic massage.
  1. Man. Therapy. Erotic massage
  I. Title
  615.8'22

ISBN 0 7137 1988 5 Paperback
ISBN 0 7137 1987 7 Hardcover

Typeset by Graphicraft Typesetters Ltd, Hong Kong.
Printed and bound in Great Britain
at The Bath Press, Avon

CONTENTS

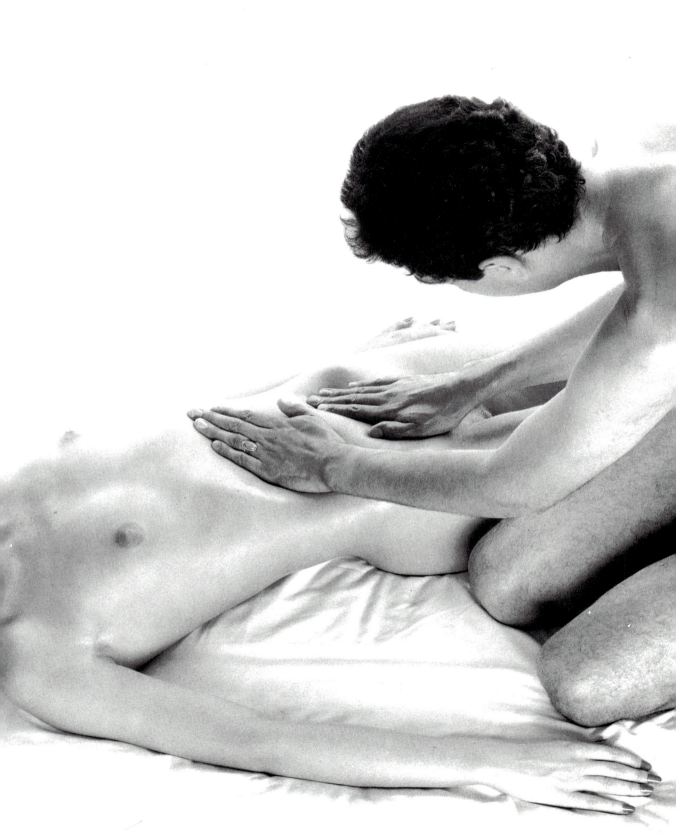

INTRODUCTION

Massage is probably one of the oldest and simplest 'treatments' known to man. It almost certainly started as simple touching and became more structured and formalised as it was found that people derived benefit from particular types of touch in different situations and conditions.

Massage also has a very distinguished history. Hippocrates, the father of medicine, wrote... 'The physician must be experienced in many things, but assuredly in rubbing... For rubbing can bind a joint that is too loose, and loosen one that is too rigid.' Pliny, the Roman naturalist, was regularly rubbed to alleviate his asthma, and Julius Caesar, who had epilepsy, was pinched all over each day to relieve neuralgia and headaches.

Eastern cultures have always considered massage to be important and for several thousand years Oriental physicians have used it as a form of healing. Shiatsu, for example, originated from Japanese massage techniques and has been enhanced by ideas gained from acupuncture and even Western techniques such as osteopathy and chiropractic.

In the Middle Ages, however, massage fell

from use in Europe, mainly because the Church taught that such pleasures of the flesh hindered an individual's spiritual growth. It wasn't until the beginning of the nineteenth century that a Swede, Per Henrik Ling, developed what we now call Swedish massage – based on his knowledge of gymnastics, and of Greek, Roman, Chinese and Egyptian techniques. In 1813 the first college offering his form of massage was founded in Stockholm and from this beginning the art and benefits of massage have become known and practised throughout the Western world.

Today, many people think of massage as a form of 'medical' treatment. And indeed it *is* used to relieve stress, tension and emotional trauma; and to heal damaged muscles and skeletal supporting tissues. But in addition to this it is now increasingly being seen as a means of communication between people who use it as a way of showing love and care, thus enriching interpersonal relationships.

Those who massage one another usually find that their relationship changes for the better. For this reason, therapists such as myself find it useful in helping couples to learn about one another and by doing so to improve their emotional and sexual lives.

Massage today has yet another role to play. In the age of AIDS, when many couples are concerned about sexual encounters that might threaten their health, some are looking for alternatives to genital penetration. Few people now talk of 'safe sex' and most realise that the best one can claim is saf*er* sex, except with a partner whose sexual history is totally known and trustworthy. In this context increasing numbers of couples find that erotic massage, perhaps ending in mutual masturbation, is the only kind of sex that is safe enough for them until they are ready to settle down with a partner whose sexual history they trust.

It is against this background of changing sexual practices that I have written this book. I hope that it will answer both the needs of those who are not yet in a stable relationship and want to feel sexually 'safe' and of those couples who have been together for many years and want to enrich their sensual and erotic life together.

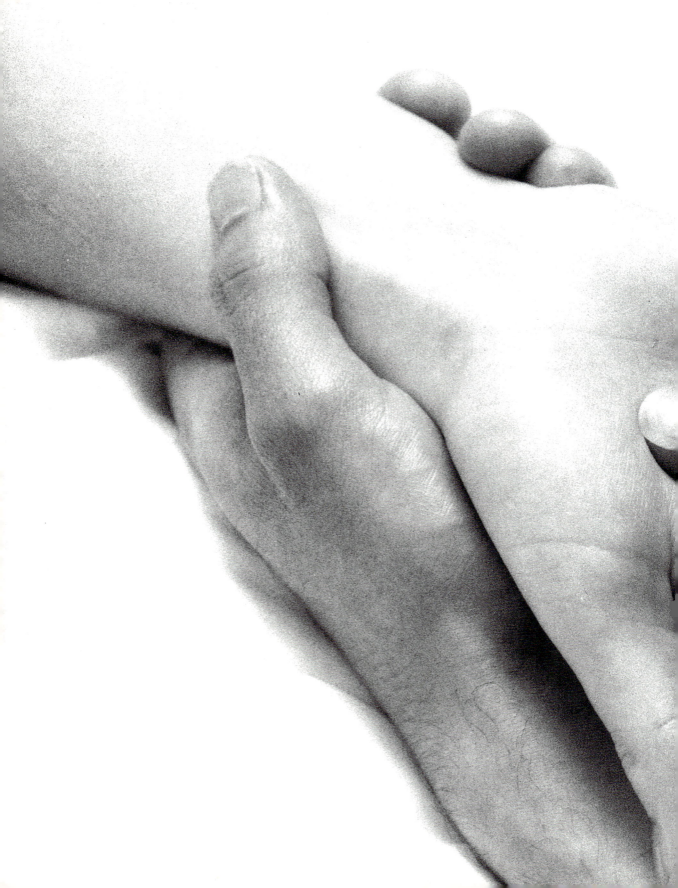

STARTING AT THE BEGINNING

What is massage?

Massage is simply a formalised, structured form of touching, so perhaps the place to start is to look at touch and see why it is so vital for human well-being.

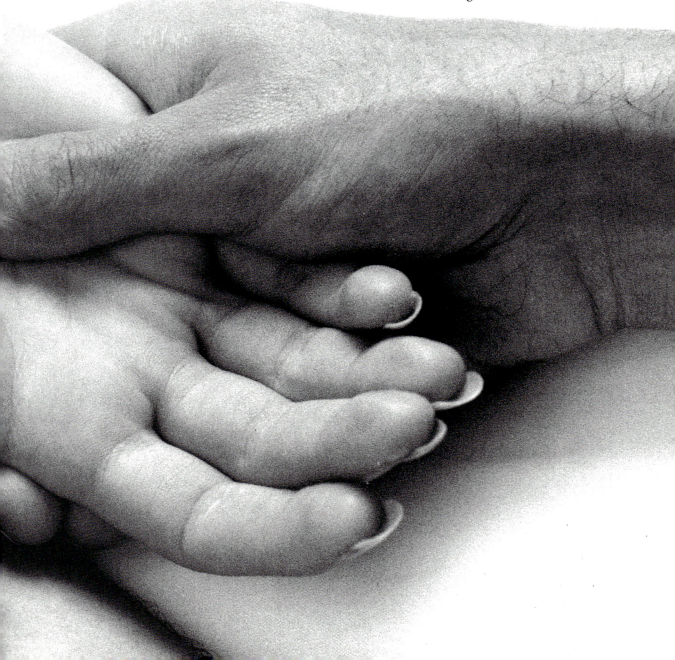

In our so-called permissive society, in which most of our senses are so richly catered for, it is amazing that the sense of touch is ignored. In fact, we live in an almost 'no-touch' society. This has come about because, over the centuries, touching others has come to be seen as having a sexual connotation.

Certainly, sex does involve touch but it is quite ridiculous to avoid all touching on the basis that a gesture might lead to sex. Alas, this is exactly what has happened in the Western world. We live in a culture that has many negative views about and prohibitions on sex, and consequently touching has come to be governed by these very same restrictions, as if touching *were* sex – which, of course, it is not.

Because many of us, once past the cradle or early childhood, touch and are touched so little we understandably find it difficult to touch others in *any* circumstances – even sexual. I see many couples who have engaged quite happily in the sexual act for years but who are intimidated by touching one another because they are unused to that particular form of intimacy. Such people can truly be said to be 'out of touch' with their bodies. Indeed, in many men the constant demand for more sex is frequently an unconscious need for touching (and being touched) and closeness. They believe, erroneously, that they should not ask for touching for its own sake and so try to make it 'respectable' by including genital activity. After all, in our culture, men aren't supposed to ask for a cuddle or a stroke!

Although no one can be absolutely sure, it appears that touch is the first sense that we develop in the womb. So touch is a primal sensation which, even in adult life, takes us back to our earliest days in the womb. This understandably makes touch very special for human beings. Indeed, the American psychologist S.M. Jourard showed that people's perceptions of how much they were touched were closely related to their sense of personal self-esteem. Most people, when they are prevented from touching and being touched, feel painfully alone and isolated. A recent US study found that people forbidden skin contact complained of such feelings. Clearly,

touch has implications for us that go far beyond making things better when we are ill – the 'medical' purpose of massage.

All kinds of pains, emotional or physical, evoke a response that usually involves touching of some kind. When a child falls over the mother lovingly 'rubs it better' and holds, kisses and cuddles her child. All of these actions convey to the child that he or she is loved and valued and probably do more good than any number of pills and potions. Doctors and nurses touch their patients, albeit in a somewhat clinical way; healers throughout history have performed the ceremony of the 'laying on of hands' and most of us feel we want to touch, hold or cuddle someone we care for when they are distressed or ill.

Touch is a vital communication system that says 'I care for you' and whether we are three or ninety-three it unconsciously takes us back to the time when we were babies in our mothers' arms. We feel safe.

Unfortunately, as we grow up we receive less and less in the way of loving, physical contact and boys especially are taught – usually quite unconsciously – by their parents, that they should be tough. They should not need or want cuddling, touching, stroking, or kissing in times of adversity. However, it is a fact that we *never* outgrow our needs for touch and in today's 'nuclear' family we have all too few people who are available to give us such attention even if they were prepared to do so. By and large it is more difficult to accept touch from a stranger and yet members of our own families may have become virtual strangers.

The least stringent anti-touch taboo is between mothers and their daughters – because they are of the same sex and it is accepted in our culture that women are by nature more emotional and caring. As a result, women fare better in adult life, being far more willing, and able, to touch one another non-sexually without feeling bad about it. Men, in contrast, can be almost phobic on the subject. Being thought to have homosexual inclinations is one of the greatest fears that many men have. Therefore, even to think of massaging another man is quite beyond the pale. Men will cuddle and caress babies, because they are said to be 'asexual'. However, as their children begin to grow up and develop more clearly defined 'sexual identities', men become increasingly ill at ease in touching them at all, for fear of being seen as sexually provocative. And adult men almost never touch one another if they can help it. This does not mean that men cease to need to be touched; rather that they find ways that are culturally sanctioned to satisfy their needs. This they do in a sexual relationship with their partner and in sporting activities where touching is permitted.

However much we try to fool ourselves, touch is so basic to our human condition that we all try to get it in whatever way we can. For example, many women who do not have a satisfying relationship with their husbands say that touching and cuddling their babies and children helps to compensate for lack of such contact in their adult relationship. Indeed, it is my professional experience that some women have more children in order to hold on to the closeness of physical touching and togetherness when their earlier offspring become more independent.

Ashley Montagu, in his book *Touching: The Human Significance of the Skin* (Harper and Row) 1971, maintains that the basic need to be touched must be satisfied if the organism is to survive. The distinguished psychologist Alexander Lowen feels that schizophrenia may come about as a result of too little touching in early life. The schizophrenic is seen as being 'out of touch' with himself. There are also studies that show links between touch deprivation in childhood and later violence.

Even this brief review of the importance of touch must convince the reader that human beings were indeed made to touch and to be touched. If this were not so, it would be unlikely that such a great proportion of our brains would be devoted to the sense of touch.

So, in answer to the question 'what is massage?'—it is simply a systematic form of touching that produces various predictable results. Let us now look more closely at the different types of massage.

Types of massage

Over the centuries, many forms of massage have been developed as methods of healing. They include:

● Aromatherapy, in which essential plant oils are rubbed into the skin to produce beneficial effects in the body.

● Shiatsu, an ancient Japanese massage system based on a knowledge of acupuncture points.

● Reflexology, a system of foot massage that has effects on other parts of the body.

● Acupressure, in which fingers—instead of needles—are used to stimulate acupuncture points.

● Touch-for-health, a system involving muscle testing.

● Swedish massage, probably the mother of all Western mainstream massage techniques.

Some of these forms of massage are considered in more detail in Chapter Five. They are not, however, the main concern of this book because we are not concentrating on therapeutic massage, meant to alleviate suffering or to cure medical ailments. This book looks at the other two areas of massage—sensual and erotic massage. These are primarily couple-centred methods of massage whose aim is the giving and receiving of pleasure rather than the curing of physical ills. Needless to say, by increasing emotional well-being, such methods do have beneficial effects on the individual's body and mind and thus could be said to be 'curative' in the widest sense of the word. Certainly, it is my personal experience that couples who massage one another feel better not just in their relationship with one another but in their own general health and sense of well-being.

Why bother with sensual and erotic massage?

Over the years many couples have asked me why they should bother with sensual and erotic massage. After all, they argue, they have a good or reasonable sex life and communicate well enough on most things, so why give themselves yet another commitment to fit into their busy lives?

I think this argument highlights what is so wrong with many man-woman relationships today. And this is why, as a marital therapist, I place such importance on learning and using these techniques, and teach them to my patients.

Sensual and erotic massage is worth taking trouble over for the following reasons:

❋ *It encourages couples to create time and space in which to be alone together.*
This is something that many do not otherwise bother to do. Most couples I see would benefit from spending much more time together, taking the trouble really to get to know one another. Many couples who *do* lots of things together and perhaps enjoy a social whirl that is the envy of others rarely spend time with one another alone, sharing and loving in the quietness of their relationship. Instead of simply *being*, they pour their energies into *doing* all the time. Far too many of us spend our lives doing rather than being. Needless to say, our relationships suffer as a result.

❋ *It costs nothing but time.*
For even the least well off couple, massage is something that they can share without financial cost. Most of us have come to think that we need to spend money in order to 'have fun'. This is not so. The old truism that the best things in life are free was never more true than in regard to massage. It is also more readily available than sex.

❋ *It isn't goal-centred.*
When couples come together for any kind of intimate activity it can end up becoming goal-centred. Men, especially, seem to have to set goals, however unconscious these may be, and women often find that this becomes tiresome or, eventually, even unacceptable. When you massage one another, however, it is enough simply to have as your goal that you please one another. There are no pressures to bring about an orgasm, and no failures due to fear. In short, the sole aim of giving or receiving a massage is pleasure for its own sake and this, unfortunately, is all too rare for most couples.

❋ *It is a fulfilling substitute for intercourse.*
Many couples, as we have seen, see sex as being the only way that they can satisfy their need for touching. This is a shame, because touching and sex are not the same thing and yet massage can be as satisfying as either – and is wonderfully beneficial when, for any of the following reasons conventional sex is difficult or not possible.

● For most couples, at the time of the month when the woman is menstruating, penis-in-vagina sex is not acceptable.

● Pregnancy can be a time for sexual abstinence for others.

● A woman who has just had a baby or a gynaecological operation will be sexually unavailable for a while.

● Anyone who is worried that he or she might have a sexually transmitted disease and especially anyone who fears that they or their partner are at risk of being HIV-positive is wise to avoid sex until they have been cleared by a doctor.

● Many thousands of women occasionally or regularly suffer from cystitis or thrush, or both, which makes it difficult or impossible to engage in sexual intercourse for a while. Herpes, too, rules out sex during an attack.

● Millions of people have sexual dysfunctions such as painful intercourse, or disorders of ejaculation or orgasm at some time in their lives together.

And so on. Instead of such couples retreating from sexual activity entirely, as many do (if they do not seek solace outside their relationship, that is), they could use sensual and erotic massage as a highly pleasurable and rewarding alternative until their usual sexual activities can be resumed. It is a tragedy that I see daily – that far too many couples behave as though their sexual lives were over at the first sign of failure, illness or disappointment. If only they knew how to touch one another in a loving and healing way in sensual and erotic massage, many an affair would be prevented and many a marriage would be enriched instead of being destroyed.

❋ *It is a valuable addition to intercourse.*
Over many years together most couples find that, sexually, they become at least a little bored with one another. They probably made love for some time before they were married and then experienced the stresses and strains of young family life, with consequent restrictions on their privacy – and opportunities to be alone together. The sparkle is lost, the sexual champagne becomes flat and many begin to think of looking elsewhere. All my clinical experience has taught me that it is usually more worthwhile to invest effort in restoring the relationship you have than to start again, and sensual and erotic massage can be a great help in making this happen.

Many couples have told me how massaging one another started them off on a totally new road after many years of thinking that they knew everything there was to know about one another. This comes about partly because, when sensitively done, massage takes the receiver back to his or her earliest days of life as they abandon themselves to the wonderful sensations. In psychological jargon this is known as 'regression' and it can have profound effects. Many say that massage puts them in touch with feelings they never knew they had; that it is a sort of mystical experience, a kind of meditation, and not just for the receiver but also for the giver.

This can mean that emotions start to be revived either at the time or afterwards, and these feelings can greatly deepen the relationship. Couples tell me that after a really loving massage session they feel closer than ever before. Indeed, it is almost impossible to feel hostile to someone who has just massaged you well and this is why couples who regularly massage one another rarely row. This basic, return-to-the-womb trust brings to most relationships enormous benefits that some people pay a fortune to achieve via professional therapy. Massage, then, can enhance a relationship that has begun to tarnish, and it does so in ways that cannot be foreseen or even believed by those who have no experience of them.

❋ *It makes sex better.*
We shall look at this benefit in detail on page 60; suffice it to say here that most couples find that by taking the pressure off 'sexual performance' they enhance their pleasure on the occasions when they *do* have sex. Many people, men in particular, use sex to achieve emotional ends that should not be reached by sex and many are delighted to be relieved of the need to 'perform'. In effect, they are being given 'permission' to enjoy non-genital closeness and intimacy.

❋ *It is the best way of improving communication.*
Few of us communicate as well as we could with our partner and sensual massage is a wonderful way of learning how to do so. We see on page 18 how this happens.

❋ *It is pleasantly relaxing.*
Many of us relax very little in today's hustle and bustle but to do a massage properly entails making time and space, and relaxing together. For many couples sex itself is not very relaxing, coloured as it is by all kinds of unconscious (and, of course, perfectly conscious) pressures such as:

● Fears of failure.
● Having to perform.
● Differences in sexual appetite.
● Differences of sexual tastes and styles.
● One partner not feeling like it when the other does.
● Fears of pregnancy.

These and a host of other hazards disturb the marital bed in most households, if only some of the time.

Sensual and erotic massage does away with all this and gives most couples a reliable way of pleasuring one another and relaxing into the bargain.

Setting the scene

You don't need much in order to be able to massage your partner. You will need to care enough to want to do it, of course. You will also need time; and a certain amount of energy and skill are vital. Also, there is a small amount of equipment that will help. But however you do it you will need to set the scene so that the experience is the best it can possibly be for both of you.

CREATING THE RIGHT ENVIRONMENT

Creating the right environment is worth effort. Of course, you can carry out a massage out of doors if it is warm enough and you have the necessary privacy, and you can do a 'quickie' massage almost anywhere that is comfortable but, for the best results, here are some tips that couples have found useful.

❊ *Take the phone off the hook.*
Most of us are at the beck and call of our telephone whether at work or at home but there's nothing so guaranteed to wreck a relaxing massage as the insistent ring of the 'phone. It usually ruins the atmosphere and, on occasions, it can be impossible to regain the lost mood that session. So, if you have an answering machine, turn down all the settings and if you can actually unplug the 'phone, do so!

❊ *If you are not alone in the house put up a 'Do not disturb' notice.*
This keeps children or other adults out, though most people tend to massage one another at night so that interruptions are not such a problem. This does, however, have another disadvantage, as both of you may be tired at the end of the day.

❊ *Dim the lights.*
Massaging one another should be relaxing, so turn off harsh lights. You need just enough illumination so that you can see what you are doing. You could fit a dimmer switch to your normal lighting or candle-light is very soothing and romantic. Some people become very adept at doing it in the dark. Indeed, ancient Oriental masseurs were often selected from the blind because their sense of touch was already so enhanced by their having to rely on it.

❊ *Warm the room.*
Ideally, the temperature should be about 75°F/ 24°C. The best form of heat is that provided indirectly by a radiator. Fan heaters are noisy and distracting and tend to create a draught of hot air over a small area. Switch on the heating at least half an hour before you intend to begin the massage session. Some people also find that they need to keep the receiver warm by putting a blanket or towel over the parts of the body not being massaged. Some couples use an electric over-blanket in the winter. However you achieve the right degree of warmth, ensure that you *are* warm whether you are giving or receiving massage. Either one or both of you can get tense muscles if you are too cold and this will hinder the massage process or even make it a waste of time.

❊ *Put on some music if this is what you like.*
Some people find music very relaxing and others, a distraction. Do not use tapes or records that have lyrics – stick to music alone for best results.

❊ *Prepare a firm surface on which to massage your partner.*
Whilst it is tempting to use the bed it is best not to do so because so much of the energy you put into the massage ends up being dissipated into the mattress. It is far better to use the floor. Put a couple of folded blankets, a pad of foam, or a sleeping bag down and cover them with a sheet. The area covered by the padding should be large enough to accept not only the receiver's body but also your own knees. If you are uncomfortable you will not be able to give a good massage and your tension and discomfort will be transmitted to the receiver.

❊ *Raise the receiver's head with a thin pillow.*
This makes the neck much more comfortable. Similarly, when the receiver is on his or her back place a small pillow under the lower legs or behind the knees; this will help the receiver's lower back to rest in a more comfortable position. As about half of the massage takes place with the receiver on his or her back, this reduces backache and makes the whole process much more relaxing.

❊ *Both giver and receiver should remove any jewellery.*
Watches, rings and body jewellery not only get in the way, they can cause pain or even damage in

certain situations. It is best therefore to remove all such items to be on the safe side.

✻ *Undress to leave as few clothes as you feel comfortable with.*

Ideally, you should both be naked – but if the room is not as warm as recommended the giver should wear light, unrestricting clothing.

Preparation

Because massage involves skin contact, cleanliness is important. Some couples like to bathe or shower together first, perhaps starting to massage one another a little in the water as a pleasant preliminary. This can be highly enjoyable if you use a loofah, shampoo brush, or bath mitt to gently massage your partner.

If you have neither the time nor the opportunity to bathe with one another do at least ensure that your hands are clean if you are the giver. And keep your fingernails short so that you cannot accidentally scratch your partner.

The hands are the main tools of the giver so take every care to keep them smooth and sensual. Keep your fingers flexible, too, if necessary by practising some kind of close work that involves fine detail such as embroidery or modelmaking. This is especially likely to be useful if you normally do manual work and your hands have become used to coarse movements. Practice makes perfect in massage, as in most skills, so do not be disheartened if initially you find that you are not as dextrous as you or your partner would like. Follow his or her guidance and you will soon begin to get it right.

Don't forget that much of the effect you'll be having will come from the natural healing that we all have in our hands. The 'laying on of hands' is an ancient practice recorded throughout history. Modern technology actually allows us to measure the healing forces and energy flowing through the hands as people concentrate on healing with them. It is thought that the energy transfer that takes place during massage is the most vital part of the procedure.

Do not massage one another after a heavy meal or if you have had much to drink; both can spoil, or even totally ruin, a massage.

Silencing your mind is also an important part of the preparation for a good massage. Try to put any troubles of the day out of your mind and concentrate deeply on what you are about to do. An absent-minded or physically exhausted giver is a real menace to the receiver who will in turn receive very little. So, fill your mind with caring compassion for your partner.

Some precautions

Massage is a natural healing method and a relaxing form of recreation yet it is not without dangers in certain situations. Never massage any areas where any of the following conditions are present:

● Fractures

● Open wounds

● Sores

● Boils

● Infectious rashes

● Easily damaged veins (especially in the legs)

● Bruises

● Lumps or tumours

● Inflamed joints

● Thrombosis or phlebitis in the legs

● Anyone who has a fever.

Where necessary seek medical help to get these sorted out before proceeding.

Giving and receiving

Although I refer throughout the book to the 'giver' and the 'receiver', in a sense this is misleading because massage is all about *sharing*. In one sense, the receiver is just as much a giver as the 'giver'. During a massage the two participants exchange energy flows and communicate intimately whatever their role in the massage session.

The receiver gives his or her trust and is totally vulnerable to the giver who, in turn, opens up all his or her channels of communication in order to be sensitive and aware of the needs of the receiver. In fact, being a receiver can be more difficult than being a giver because most of us find it more difficult to be totally relaxed, passive and vulnerable than to be 'doing'.

If you are the receiver, allow yourself to become totally passive. Shut off your awareness of the outside world; focus, perhaps, on a pleasurable scene and really live through it. Close your eyes and focus on your breathing or what is being done to you. Or even empty your mind totally. The only 'duty' of the receiver is to let the giver know if certain parts of the massage are more – or less – enjoyable and to lovingly guide him or her as and when necessary. At first this will mean talking (see below) but after a while your partner will know what your needs are by your responses: the little moans, groans, sighs, subtle body movements and so on that you make as the massage progresses.

If you are the giver your role is to be open to what your partner wants and best enjoys and then to fulfil his or her wishes. We shall now see how this can best be achieved.

Communicating through touch

Many of us think that the only way to communicate with out partner is to talk. But this isn't necessarily always the case. We communicate all the time, and often without talking. Non-verbal communication is probably responsible for more of what goes on between human beings than is talking. In spite of this many couples I see are rather bad at reading the cues from one another.

This is where sensual massage comes in useful. By really listening to your partner early on as you learn what he or she best likes you not only encourage openness but learn how to get it right for him or her. The only responsibility of the giver is to make the massage really pleasurable for the receiver, whatever this takes. This usually means discarding all kinds of pre-conceived ideas

as the receiver re-defines what you *thought* he or she liked.

All of this give and take is extremely helpful in a couple's sexual life because most will come to behave in bed in the same way as they do on the massage mat. Remember, it is not enough to make assumptions on which you then structure your massage; you must be guided by your partner's expressed needs at the time. A willingness to be flexible and to throw out old notions of what 'should' be pleasant will bring great benefit to your sexual life as you transfer similar communication skills and openness to the bedroom.

As time goes by, perhaps after as few as six sessions, you will be so good at 'reading' your partner that talk will become unnecessary. You will be able to communicate at a much deeper level, reading quite subtle body language that before would have gone unheeded.

I believe that couples who massage one another also become more spiritually attuned. They start to communicate on a higher plane both when they are massaging one another and when they are not. This can only be to their advantage.

However, communicating at this level when massaging your partner does take practice, knowledge and skill. Here are some tips on how to give a massage.

❊ Start off by lying down next to one another either flat on the floor or bed, or lying in the 'spoons' position on your side with your front against your partner's back. Synchronize your breathing so that you breathe in and out at the same time. Relax and lose yourselves in this togetherness.

❊ Remember that the sort of massage I am describing in this book is about relaxing and feeling safe and trusting. This feeling of trust must never be broken: never let your partner down. This means always supporting the part being massaged. Even if your partner falls asleep, he or she should be able to feel totally confident that they are in good hands. Handle each part of the body as though it were extremely precious to you – as I hope that it is.

❋ If you are the giver, before you start ask your partner if there are any particular parts of his or her body that feel in special need of attention.

❋ Balance your body so that your torso is mainly upright and straight. Let your shoulders hang loose and be sure that you are not tense as you do the massage. Any tension comes across to the receiver and can ruin a massage.

❋ Focus your attention on your partner and put all other thoughts out of your mind. Concentrate on your hands as you massage and always be open to what he or she wants.

❋ A good massage should feel like one continuous sequence, so take care you always have one hand in contact with the receiver's body to ensure this continuity.

❋ Keep the strokes reliably smooth and rhythmic. Work slowly and your partner will get the best out of the massage. There should be no surprises for the receiver — just a flow of predictably enjoyable strokes and movements.

All of these things will help to create the right mood and ensure that true communication takes place. Sensual and erotic massage have nothing in common with fixing the car and are largely intuitive processes of sharing, involving a total commitment to what you are doing and to the person with whom you are sharing the experience.

What you will need

Unless you want to invest in a proper massage table, and few couples do, the only things you will need are some oil or powder with which to lubricate the skin and perhaps a few pieces of special equipment to make the massage more enjoyable. Let us look at these in more detail.

OILS

Oils are used when massaging simply to make the contact between the skin and your hands more free from friction and thus more pleasant for the receiver as your hands glide over his or her skin.

The same effect can be obtained using talcum powder if you prefer not to oil the skin.

It is easy to overestimate how much oil is needed; a very small amount is sufficient to lubricate the skin. If you are too lavish, the oil will run over the contours of the body and onto the sheet underneath. Too much oil also *reduces* the amount of contact you can make, which is in itself a disadvantage.

Once you have oiled one part of the body (oil each part only when you are ready to massage it rather than all at once), that application should be sufficient for the whole massage, except when working on big areas such as the back, or very hairy zones — especially in men.

What sort of oil you use is up to you but do not feel that you must use fancy oils. You do not need to spend a fortune. Any vegetable oil, such as sunflower, safflower, or coconut is perfectly acceptable. Many beauty shops and even high-street chemists now sell inexpensive massage oils. You could even use olive oil but it is thicker and sticky. Mineral oils such as baby oil can also be used but they are not absorbed into the skin well.

Best of all, but most expensive, are aromatherapy oils. These are scented and can be tailor-made to have very specific effects — for example, they can be relaxing, invigorating, or erotic.

One company in the UK makes a plain massage oil that can be used as the base for your own personalised product. Simply add a few drops of your favourite perfume.

Some people like to keep their oil in a dish but this can easily spill in use, so a flip-top bottle is best. This gives peace of mind whilst you are concentrating on the massage itself. Always warm the oil before starting, by putting the bottle into a bowl of hot water or by standing it a safe distance from a radiator.

When using the oil *never* put it onto your partner's skin direct from the bottle, because it can tickle unpleasantly or be cold. Always pour a little of the warmed oil into your hand first and then place that hand on your partner's body. Let it rest there for a moment and then slowly start to spread the oil over the area to be massaged. Make sure that your hands are relaxed and floating over the surface of your partner's skin. When making contact allow them to fall as if they were feathers. Similarly, when breaking contact with the skin do so gently and smoothly, never jerkily.

When you have finished the entire massage, your partner's body will be slightly oiled all over. Have a small towel handy to remove the excess or use surgical spirit to wash it off.

EQUIPMENT

An electric vibrator is a useful tool for massage but be sure to use it before you start the massage proper. Although they have become associated with sexual arousal, vibrators can be useful for their original purpose! Even the phallic-shaped ones designed for clitoral stimulation can be good for short bursts of massaging. The best, though, are the electrically operated ones that can be attached to the back of your hand, so that it is your hand rather than the plastic or rubber of the gadget that makes contact with the body.

It is possible to buy numerous types of massage equipment and most of the large electrical companies have their own version. 'Personal massagers' have different heads that can be interchanged for use on various parts of the body. While many women (and some men) use them for sexual arousal they also make fine massagers and if you have no partner or your partner is unavailable, you can use them to give yourself a massage.

A sauna or Jacuzzi can be a wonderful addition to your massage routine but most of us have neither the money nor the space for such luxuries. A really good bath is worth investing in though because if it is large enough you can bathe together as a lead-up to your massage. A power shower is within the reach of many families and this can be a good form of preliminary water massage before progressing to the real thing.

Various body rollers and similar devices are available from specialist health shops, chemists, spas and hydros and they, too, are worth experimenting with.

For the vast majority of couples, however, massage can be wholly satisfying as a person-to-person affair in which they use only their hands.

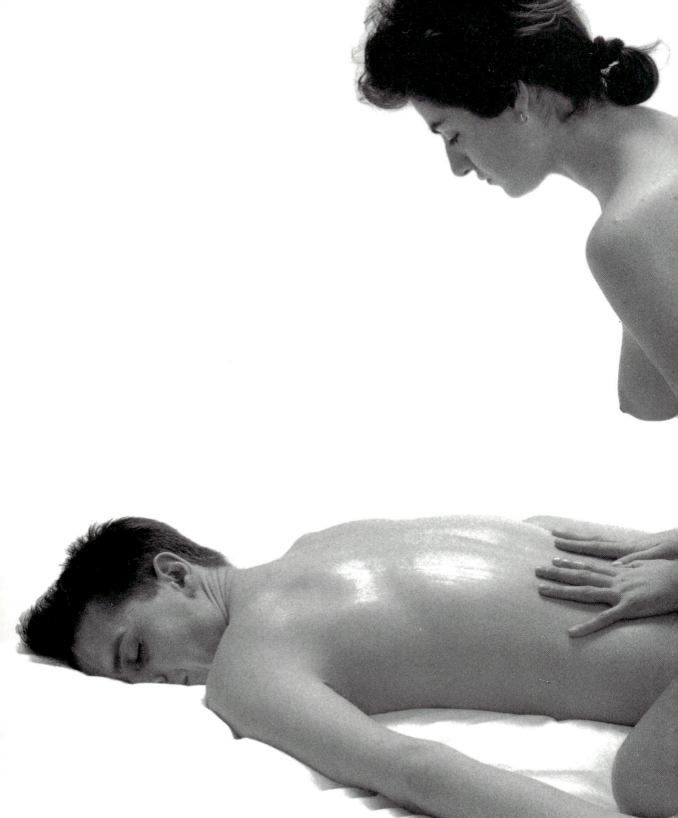

2

SOME BASIC STROKES AND TECHNIQUES

The main thing to remember, when massaging your partner, is that your intuitive feelings should be your guide rather than anything written here.

There is no right or wrong way to massage, do whatever feels good for the receiver and then patiently learn how to make it even better. Most couples gradually improvise their own methods—techniques that particularly suit them—and it is certainly *not* essential to become an 'expert' at massage. However, it helps to learn certain basic skills so that you can both get the best out of the sessions you share together.

Many of my couples are delighted to learn some formal skills because this opens new doors for them. What at first may seem a chore to learn soon becomes natural and, like driving, becomes second nature once you are experienced. The actual manual skills then function automatically, leaving you free to enjoy the giving and receiving. So, if at first it seems like rather a lot to think about, don't panic—you will be surprised how quickly you improve, with practice.

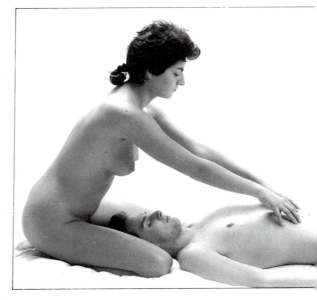

There are literally thousands of ways of touching your partner but here let us first look at the techniques that are useful for sensual massage. (Erotic massage, discussed on pages 57–116, calls for rather different methods.)

It is useful to think of the basic sensual massage strokes and movements in three main groups: gliding, medium-deep, and deep. A fourth category—percussion—will also be described but I do not find that many couples use it much.

Gliding

These strokes are some of the most sensual, and are easy to do. You simply let your hands glide gently and rhythmically over the surface of your partner's skin. Use these movements to start and to finish a massage session, by making them large and expansive rather than focused on a particular area.

Such movements are very smooth and soothing, and for this reason are used to apply oil at the start of work on any particular area. You can do them with the flat of your hand applied to the skin and with your fingers spread apart or close together. The feelings are quite different, depending on which method you choose. If you lift your palm off the skin and just use your fingertips you can do a stroke called feathering—or butterfly strokes. This gives a lot of pleasure but requires some practice because early on it is easy inadvertently to tickle your partner and so spoil their relaxation.

Using the fingertips of both hands at the same time, or of each hand alternately, run them lightly over the skin. Travel down along the length of the body with these light brush strokes, perhaps overlapping your hands as you use first one and then the other. This is a useful stroke with which to end the massage session or to end work on any one part.

Long stroking movements are nice, too. In these you place your hands flat on your partner's body and then lean forward to slide them down (or up) the receiver's body as far as you can reach. Then circle your hands around and make the return journey. In this way you can cover large circuits of flat areas of the body, such as the chest, stomach, torso, or back.

Try making big circles with your hands one after the other, each overlapping the track of the previous hand so that they each form only part of the circumference of the circle. Many people say this feels almost magical.

Experiment with different speeds and pressures of all these strokes to see what your partner best enjoys. It is a good idea to practise on yourself first to get the hang of what different strokes feel like, and to get the pressure right.

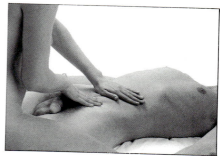

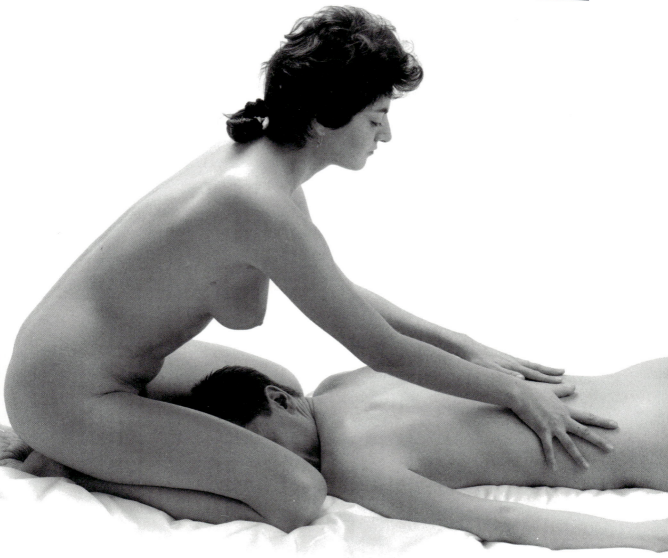

Medium-depth strokes

These use more pressure than gliding movements but do not go very deep into the muscles. A good one to start with is kneading. In this you take a 'fistful' of flesh with one hand and squeeze it as if you were kneading dough. Then release it, at the same moment grasping a similar amount of flesh close by with your other hand, and so on. Make sure that one hand is always squeezing so that contact with your partner is uninterrupted.

Another stroke worth trying is a gentle wringing action, as if your partner's body were a large towel to be wrung out. Place your hands on either side of, say, the trunk and then bring your hands together quite firmly so that both come to lie in the centre of the back. Now change hands so that the one that was pulling is now pushing, but from the other side of the body. This stroke works best on the torso but can also be used on the thighs.

A real favourite is a special form of pulling. Kneel at the side of your partner with your knees close to his or her body. Lean across and place both your hands on the opposite side of your partner's trunk, high up under the arm. Pull firmly on your right hand, drawing it towards the front of the chest and stopping just before you reach the nipple. Now do the same with your left hand, at the same time lifting off your right hand and returning it to the starting position but a little lower down the body. Continuing to use right and left hands alternately, gradually work your way down the body, overlapping the tracks you have just made until you reach the knee. Stop here and, returning to your starting point on the chest, begin the movements again.

Deep strokes

Harder to do and more tiring to perform, these call for some strength or the use of your body weight if you are slight. Because it is easy for these highly rewarding strokes to tire the giver, technique is more important here.

Never start off with these deep strokes. Always begin with gentle, soothing and relaxing movements. Once you have gained the confidence and trust of your partner you can progress to the deeper strokes. From my experience these are likely to call for much more feedback because you will be more likely to produce adverse sensations if you become too enthusiastic.

Having said this, many people are surprised by just how hardy the body is. Be guided in part by

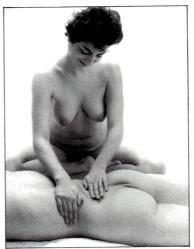
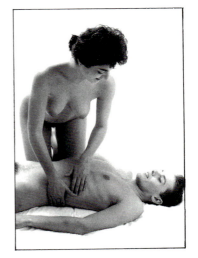

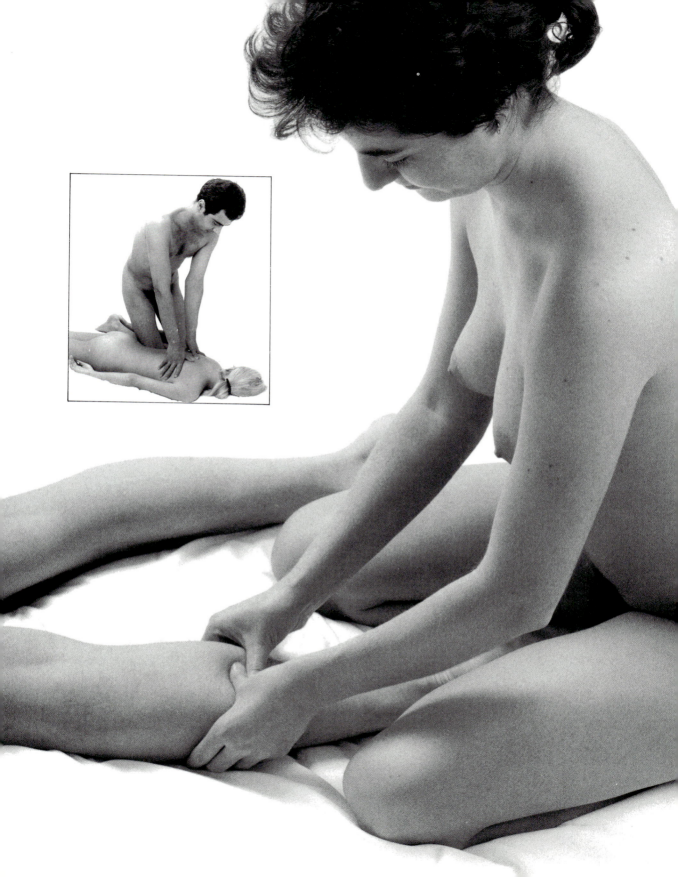

the amount of fat and muscle your partner has. Obviously a small, light person will be more easily hurt accidentally than one with a fair covering of fat and muscle, but common sense and some feedback during the first few sessions should quickly sort out such matters.

While talking about experiencing or inflicting pain during massage, there is sometimes a delicate balance to be held between just enough firmness to make the stroke feel really good and going over the barrier into real pain. Again, experience will teach both of you just where this barrier is over your first few sessions together.

Perhaps the most popularly used of the deep strokes is that using the thumbs. Press the balls of your thumbs deep into the flesh, and using small circles, short strokes, or whatever you find best for each particular part of the body, push the skin away from you. Use the thumbs together or alternately and slowly work your way across the given area in a slow, creeping movement. Always keep one thumb in contact with the skin. A variant of this is to do the same massage but using the heel of your hand instead of your thumbs.

Fingertip pressure can be very effective, if tiring for the giver. Keep the tips of your fingers together, bunching them so that they form a multi-fingered pad of tissue. Push them deeply into the flesh and seek out any tense or painful areas that your partner tells you may need this form of relief. Get your body weight behind the movement and keep your arms straight or you will soon feel exhausted. It is possible, instead, to use just one finger, for specific well-defined points of tenderness or tension, but few people can keep this up for long.

Sensitive fingertip movements are good around joints, at the top of the back (around the shoulder blade), in the palm of the hand, and on the sole of the foot. Try them out on other areas.

Percussion

This is less popular with couples doing sensual massage than with true masseurs, because this form of massage is stimulating rather than relaxing. However, it can be helpful.

Hacking is a form of percussion in which the sides of the hands alternately hit the receiver's body in a rhythmical way, all the time moving around the area being massaged. This works well on the buttocks, the thighs and the calves but can be painful elsewhere.

Pummelling is really hitting your partner with a loosely-clenched fist. Again, it should only be done in areas where there is plenty of flesh. Never do it near or over bony areas, such as the ribcage or the front of the leg.

Pinching can be surprisingly pleasurable, too. Pinch small lumps of flesh with the fingertips of each hand in turn.

Sometimes these more invigorating techniques are useful as you proceed from sensual massage to erotic massage, if that is what you intend to do at any one session. They can easily lead on to foreplay.

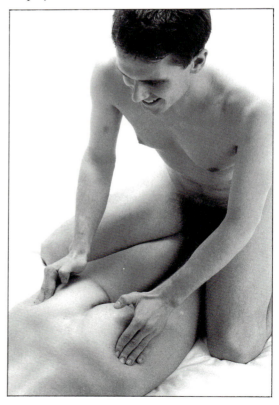

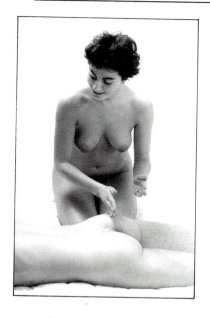
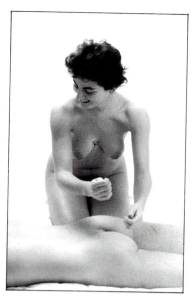
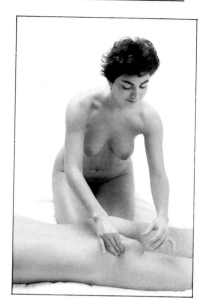

If you master all of these strokes over just a few sessions and quickly come to know what your partner best likes, you will have done extremely well. It can take months to become an expert at recognising your partner's needs and, of course, these will change from time to time. Women, especially, have differing needs according to the time of the month. This is particularly true of women who retain a lot of fluid in their tissues during the menstrual cycle. A manoeuvre that was highly exciting and enjoyable earlier in the month can become painful in the week before a period. Learning about such considerations makes a man more sensitive to his partner's body and its cyclical changes, and this greatly helps their sex life in general.

Having learned and mastered your basic strokes, keep on practising and developing your own variations. Those I have described work well for most people but there is considerable scope for individual variation. This is a point worth making again and again because I find that some people, when massaging their partner, often concentrate on the areas and stroke types that they themselves best enjoy. Some find it difficult to believe that their partner enjoys something different and may even get quite annoyed because

they cannot force their preference onto their partner. This usually tells me a lot about the marriage and, indeed, the couple also learn greatly from talking it through.

You, too, can learn from how you communicate during a massage. Use the experience to see how well you actually listen to one another's requests and needs. How *do* you respond? How do you feel when you are asked to do something, especially if it is not what you think you should do or would prefer to do? Are you tense or anxious at having to receive? Do you find yourself always offering to give and rarely receiving? All of these, and many more, are useful areas for discussion within a loving relationship.

Many people of both sexes actually censor pleasure. It is as if they have been brought up to believe that it is wrong to feel good – and indeed many of them have. Such a person will need a lot of patient understanding from their partner to help them break free from such ingrained inhibitions and to allow their feelings of pleasure to come through. Try to be positive in your reaction to any such issues that arise as a result of massaging one another and seek professional help if things get too difficult for the two of you to handle alone.

3

HOW TO DO A BASIC SENSUAL MASSAGE

There is no absolute right or wrong way of doing a sensual massage, as I have said before, but however you decide to do it you will need to be systematic about it if you do not want to miss out whole areas of pleasure for your partner.

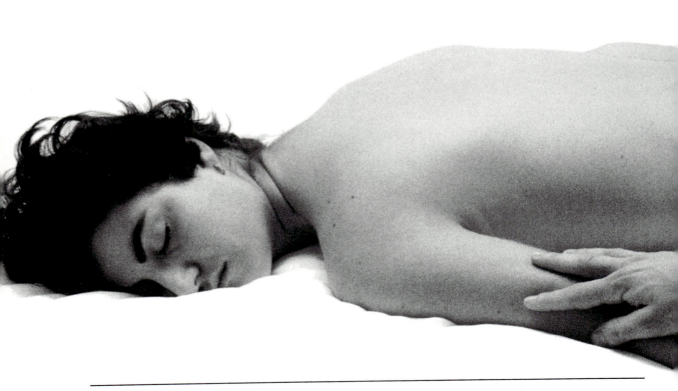

Having said this, it also depends on how much time you have at your disposal. Many massage books – and there are some good ones around – are written with the assumption that the couple has an hour or two to spend. If this *is* so you could work through the whole of the sequence described below; it takes about an hour to do thoroughly. However, if you have only half that time or even less, it does not mean that you have to put off giving and receiving until another day. Ask your partner what he or she would like best and then do a shortened version of the massage routine. A loving couple should feel free to ask for, and receive, what they want, whether this happens to be a back massage, ten minutes devoted to their feet, or whatever. It most certainly does *not* have to be 'the whole production' or nothing.

Some of the things described below will be especially pleasant for certain individuals and yet for others may be positively unpleasant. Over the first few weeks of trying things out you will soon discover what you both like. The routine I describe below is somewhat full and I know very few couples who do it all every time. Nor should they, necessarily.

Giving and receiving a good massage has nothing in common with, say, following a cookery recipe. You do not have to follow a plan slavishly in order to be successful. In fact it is far better if you don't stick rigidly to a set routine. Early on, though, as when learning most things, it pays to be systematic and structured about it all. Later you will be able to take matters into your own hands and devise tailor-made sequences for your partner.

There is, however, one rule worth following. Do not touch the breasts or genitals in the course of a massage. A sensual massage is not aimed at sexual arousal – in fact arousal can detract from the pleasure. If, once you have completed your sensual massage, you want to go on to erotic massage or foreplay then, of course, the breasts and genitals will become centres of attention.

From my experience, the best place to start a massage is the back. So let's look at this first.

The back

I suggest to couples that they start with back massage for many reasons.

● It is a relatively strong, flat part of the body, which makes it a good starting point while the giver gets into the mood and the receiver starts to relax and trust the giver.

● It is large and responds to many different types of strokes, thus allowing the giver to introduce variety into his or her repertoire – and produce good feelings for the receiver right from the start.

● Many people are very tense at the top of their neck and shoulders and doing something about this is a good start to a more generalised body massage.

● Back massage often makes the receiver so relaxed that he or she is then ready for the rest of the procedure to follow.

● Lastly – and perhaps as a therapist I see more of this than others do – if the individual being massaged lies face down at the beginning of a massage, he or she feels less vulnerable than lying face-up, particularly if naked.

All of these reasons make the back a good place to start.

First, the giver should get into a good, relaxed position. Because the back is so large, especially if the receiver is both tall and well built, you will be moving about quite a bit when doing long strokes. This can best be achieved by kneeling at the head of the receiver, who is lying face down, flat on the floor, arms lying along his or her sides and the hands/palms upwards. The head should be turned to one side. Your knees are either side of the receiver's head in this position.

Another favourite of mine is for the giver to 'sit' astride the receiver's buttocks but taking care not to put any weight onto the receiver's body. This improves the sensuality of the massage because the giver's body is so intimately in contact with that of the receiver.

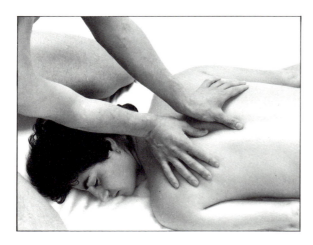

Now you are ready to start the actual massage.

First, take a few slow, deep breaths in and out, at the same time relaxing your shoulders. Close your eyes if this helps and centre your thoughts on your partner.

Then open your eyes and taking a little warmed oil in the palm of one hand lightly spread it all over your partner's back. Then close your eyes once more while you concentrate on the feel of the body beneath your hands. Do some long strokes up and down the back making large circles with both hands, each making the same movements but in a mirror image of one another.

Now, opening your eyes again, you are ready to work more firmly, using whatever strokes you find best, on the base of the neck, then the shoulders. Do one shoulder at a time and use kneading, thumb pressure and broad strokes thoroughly to massage the top of the back, seeking out any knotted or 'gritty-feeling' areas. Work all around the shoulder blades, perhaps with the tips of your fingers, and then lift the shoulder with one hand while you continue the massage of this area. For this last part you will find it best to alter your position so that you are beside the receiver's chest and facing his or her head.

Now straddle him or her as before and, using your fingertips bunched together to form a pad, run them up and down the sides of the spine along the large muscles there.

Run your hands right from the base of the spine to the top of the back and then down again. Be guided by what feels good to your partner. Many people find that massaging certain areas produces exquisitely lovely sensations. Concentrate on such areas with deep, deliberate strokes. Then gently 'walk' your fingers up and down the spinal muscles; take great care to avoid pressure on the spines of the vertebrae in the mid-line because this can be very uncomfortable.

End with some broad, integrating strokes that 'smooth over' the whole back area.

So that you can massage the lower back with ease, reposition your body so that your knees are level with the receiver's thighs. Do some medium-deep circular movements with the hands overlapping their tracks around the base of the receiver's back. Go on to knead the buttocks, perhaps with the addition of some chopping movements, if the receiver likes this. With you at the receiver's side, leaning across to his or her opposite side, pulling up the sides of the buttocks can be good, too. However, you may prefer to leave this until later and work all down the receiver's side, as described on page 35.

Make your hands broad and using big, circular motions, massage all over the buttocks from the lower back to the top of the thighs.

Now use your bunched fingertips again to probe deeply into the muscles of the buttocks, over the hip joint. Make small circles here until you find what is most pleasurable for your partner; such sensations here can come as a great surprise at first.

Now you should be ready to start on the legs.

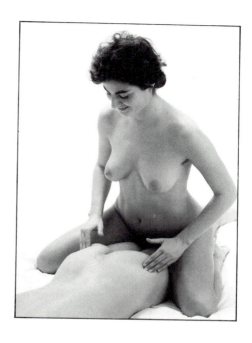

The backs of the legs

The best position in which to massage the legs is to open your partner's legs so that there is enough room for you to kneel between his or her feet and facing the body. Start by oiling both legs at once. This might mean leaning forwards if your partner is tall. When both legs are oiled from buttocks to ankles, concentrate on one leg at a time.

The backs of the legs give very variable pleasure to different people. Some like their calves massaged yet get little or no sensation on the back of the thighs, and for a few it is the other way around. Whatever you do and however you do it, always bear in mind that it is best to apply very little pressure on the skin of the legs as you go *down* them. This is because it is easy to force blood into the valves that are arranged all along the veins in the legs and this causes pain or discomfort. It can also be dangerous if the individual being massaged has varicose veins, so, if there *are* varicose veins (these are fat, knotted, tortuous and easily visible) keep your massage well clear of them.

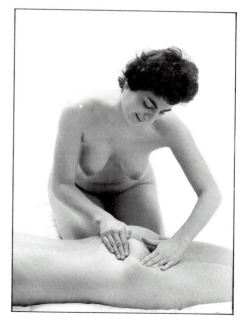

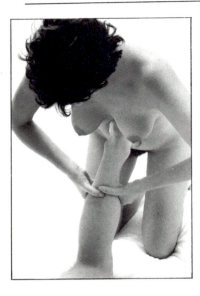
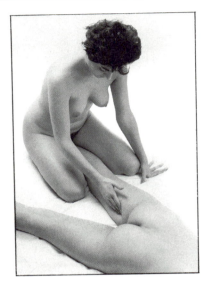
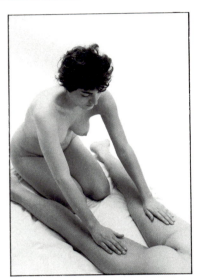

Kneading and wringing (see page 26) are good on the legs and two that I find go down well are the following:

With your partner still in the first position, raise his or her lower leg to a right angle with the floor. Sit forward and rest the sole of the receiver's foot flat against your chest, then massage the calf deeply, using both thumbs. Work up the calf firmly and repeat the movement in waves with both thumbs at the same level on the leg. Many people find this exquisitely sensuous.

Another favourite is to massage the insides of your partner's thighs. Sit comfortably astride his or her legs, level with the knees. Now massage deeply along the inner surfaces of the thighs up to, but not including, the genitals. This massage is usually very relaxing, especially for women.

Lastly, do some big, broad strokes from ankle to buttocks, running your hands over the buttocks and around the hips in large, circular movements.

Some people like to go on to the feet at this point but I find that it is easier to massage the feet when the receiver is on his or her back.

Before your partner turns over, do some gentle, preliminary work on the arms.

The backs of the arms

Kneel at the side of your partner and do some long, flat-handed strokes down the arm on that side. Start at the shoulder and caress the arm with both hands alternately in a wave-like motion as they progress down the arm. Carry the stroke right down to the fingers and end the stroke at the fingertips very sensitively. Try to envelop the whole arm with these long strokes . . . the effect is wonderful.

Lastly, kneel between your partner's legs again, or sit over the backs of his or her knees, now close together, and do some long integrating strokes all over the back of the body from neck to knees. You can also go down the arms again if you like and can reach. This unites all the areas you have been massaging and ends this phase.

Some people stop here if this is all they have time for or if there is insufficient time for the giver to become the receiver as would be the case if the whole sequence in this chapter were to be done in its entirety. Let us assume, however, that you are continuing as the giver and your partner as the receiver. The next step is to ask him or her to turn over.

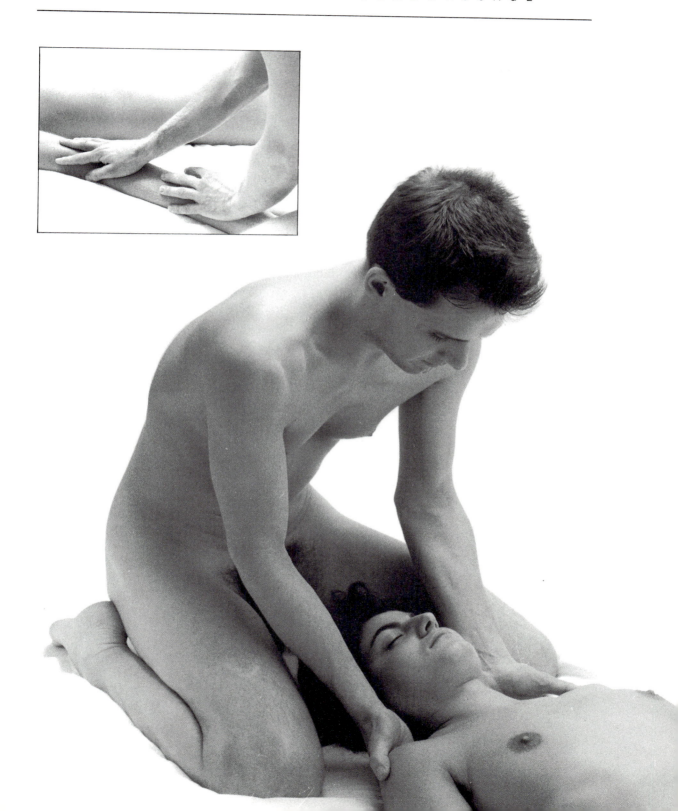

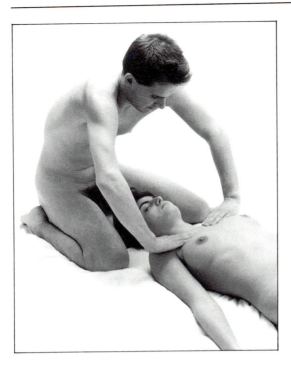

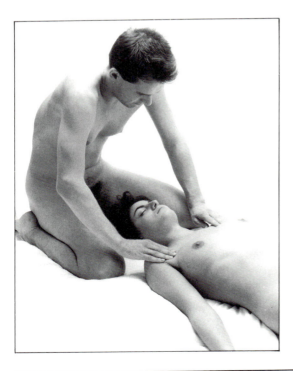

The shoulders and neck

Once your partner is lying face upwards it makes sense to go back to the neck and shoulders because they are often still tense, even if your previous efforts were beneficial. Working on the shoulders and neck from the front (as in the lower picture on p. 37) can actually be more effective because the receiver's own weight assists your efforts. Kneel at your partner's head for this part of the message.

Start, as always, by lightly oiling the area. With a little warmed oil on the palms of both your hands, begin by placing them on your partner's chest at the very top of the breasts. Let them rest there for a while with the fingertips of both your hands nearly touching one another over the breastbone. Now move the heels of your hands outwards towards the shoulders and then around the back of them to the top of the shoulder blades. Now run them up the back of the neck. Repeat this stroke several times, starting at the top of the chest each time.

Next, take hold of your partner's head with your fingers at the base of his or her skull and gently pull the neck so as to stretch it. There is no danger in this, provided you do it gently. An extension of this is gently to stretch the neck forwards by inclining it slightly towards the feet, all the time stretching the neck. Then carefully lower the head onto the floor again and place your hands under the neck. Massage the back of the neck with one hand on one side and then, reversing the process, massage the other side of the neck with your other hand.

Lastly, massage the top of the back, above the shoulder blades and out to the tip of the shoulder but this time from underneath. You did something similar earlier, when your partner was lying on his or her stomach, but this way round is particularly pleasant to do and their body weight pressing on to your hands helps greatly.

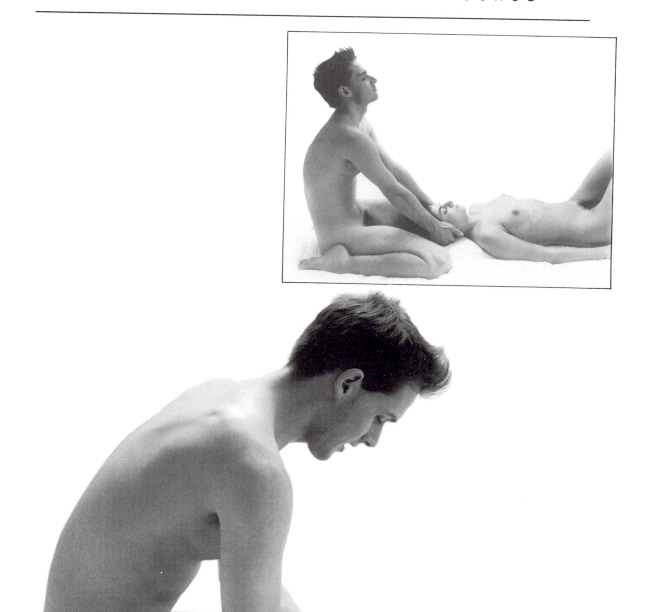

Spinal stretch

Unless your partner is very heavy or large (in which case you will find it difficult or impossible to do) this is a very enjoyable manoeuvre for the receiver.

He or she should raise their head and back a little, so that you can get your hands and arms underneath. You then lean forward so that your body is virtually parallel with your partner's and reach right down to put your hands under his or her back and sides, level with the navel.

Now tell your partner to relax totally and go floppy on you. Keeping your hands still where they are, pull back with your body weight. This pulls on the lower half of your partner's body, which is fixed by its own weight. This feels lovely for the receiver.

Now let the surface friction between your skin and your partner's slip a little and allow your hands to glide up the back of his or her spine, along the big muscles at either side of the vertebrae. Allow your hands to travel right up the receiver's back as far as the shoulders, then on to the neck and lastly right up to the scalp. This produces a very unusual sensation which most people greatly enjoy.

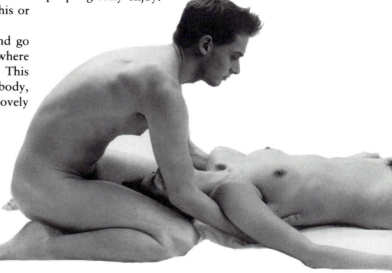

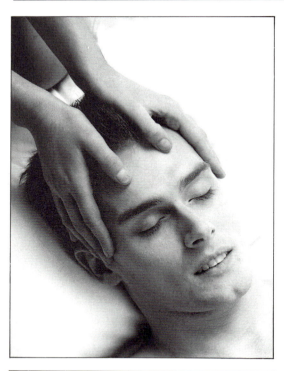

The face

Our face often reveals more of how we feel than does any other part of our body. Certainly, it is possible to read a lot from people's faces, both of their present and their past.

In my view, massaging the face is a fairly intuitive matter and calls for some experimentation to determine what feels good for your particular partner. You will not need to oil your hands again, because the small amount of oil you will need will already be on them, from the massage you have already carried out.

Sit or kneel with your partner's head between your knees and gently explore what feels nice for him or her. The face is fairly bony and firm, except over the cheeks, but don't worry about doing any damage; it is nothing like as vulnerable as it may look except for the fine skin around the eyes – be careful here. You could perhaps first try massaging your own face to get the hang of how it feels.

However, people experience very different sensations when their face is being massaged so it pays to listen carefully to the feedback from your partner while you are still learning.

Obviously, movements have to be small and controlled compared with those made when massaging the large areas of the body but you will soon become competent. Make your movements slow, too, and very soothing.

Although massaging the face satisfactorily calls for quite a lot of experience if it is to be massaged according to your partner's wishes, here are a few movements that many people find pleasant.

First place your fingertips at the sides of your partner's head (near the temples) and your thumbs centrally on his or her forehead, at the hairline. Slide your thumbs apart slowly, towards the sides of the forehead, then return them to the centre, but moving down a little, and repeat the process. Then, keeping your hands in much the same position, work on your partner's eyebrows in the same way.

Next, starting under the inner corners of the eyes work your thumbs outwards over the cheeks

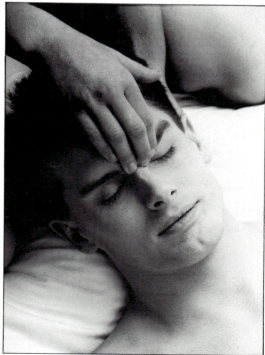

to the jawbone. Move down the cheeks as you repeat this until the whole of the lower face has been covered.

Bunch your fingertips together and massage the chewing muscles up to the jaw joint, in front of the ear. Then massage the chin with gentle pinching movements.

Using the flat of your hands, message the face all over, holding it in positions that are pleasant for your partner.

Finally, simply hold your hands over the receiver's face as a soothing end to the massage of this area.

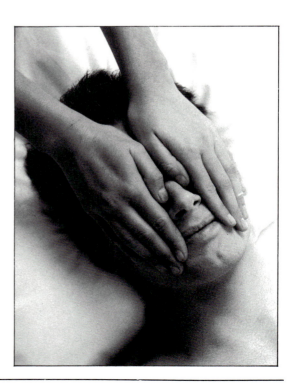

The arms and hands

Massage of the arms and hands can be a valuable experience for those who tend to bottle up their emotions. Perhaps they find themselves clenching their fists, fiddling with things, drumming their fingers, or even wanting to hit out at someone they feel angry with. All of these emotions remain 'tied up' in the arms and hands and great benefit will be derived from the release of these tensions.

Kneel beside your partner and lightly oil the arm from shoulder to hand, using your hands alternately in long, flowing strokes that overlap and work slowly down from shoulder to hand as you do this.

Just as I described for raising the foot and bending the knee on page 36 so, too, it is very relaxing for the receiver if you do the same with the arm. Raise your partner's forearm so that it rests on the elbow and hold his or her hand in one of yours. Enclose the wrist in your other hand and slowly but firmly move your hand down the forearm, squeezing it all the time as if you were milking fluid out of it. Repeat this several times as in the top picture overleaf.

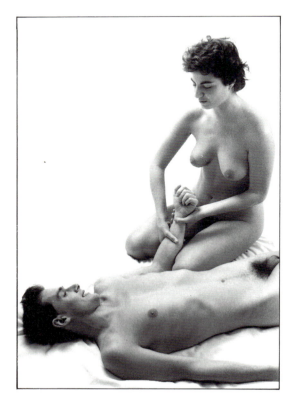

Next you can either knead or wring the upper arm. End with some long, integrating strokes of the whole arm and shoulder. Then repeat the whole process with the other arm.

The hand, too, is a remarkably enjoyable part of the body to have massaged yet it almost always comes as a surprise to people just how good it feels.

Start by asking your partner to rest his or her hand, palm up, on the floor then massage the palm gently. Then lift it up and, while holding it in one of your hands, use the thumb of your other hand to massage all over your partner's palm, asking as you do so where it feels best. Keep on exploring the palm until you have discovered all of the pleasurable areas and how he or she best likes them to be massaged. This can take some time. Indeed, like the feet (see page 52), some people enjoy having their hands massaged for many minutes.

Now gently pull the fingers one at a time; be careful about this because the sensation can be a little alarming at first. Go gently so as not to cause tension or pain. Work first on one hand and then on the other while holding the hand at the wrist firmly and securely.

Next, place your palm against that of your partner's so that your fingers match up. Now slide your fingers between his or hers and bring them upwards to your partner's fingertips. This delicious massage strokes the sides of the fingers and many people enjoy having this done for some time. Indeed, I have found that some people cannot get enough of these hand movements, so pleasurable are they.

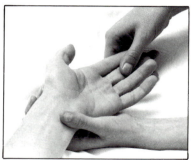
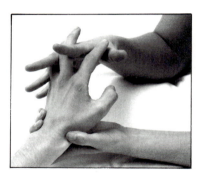

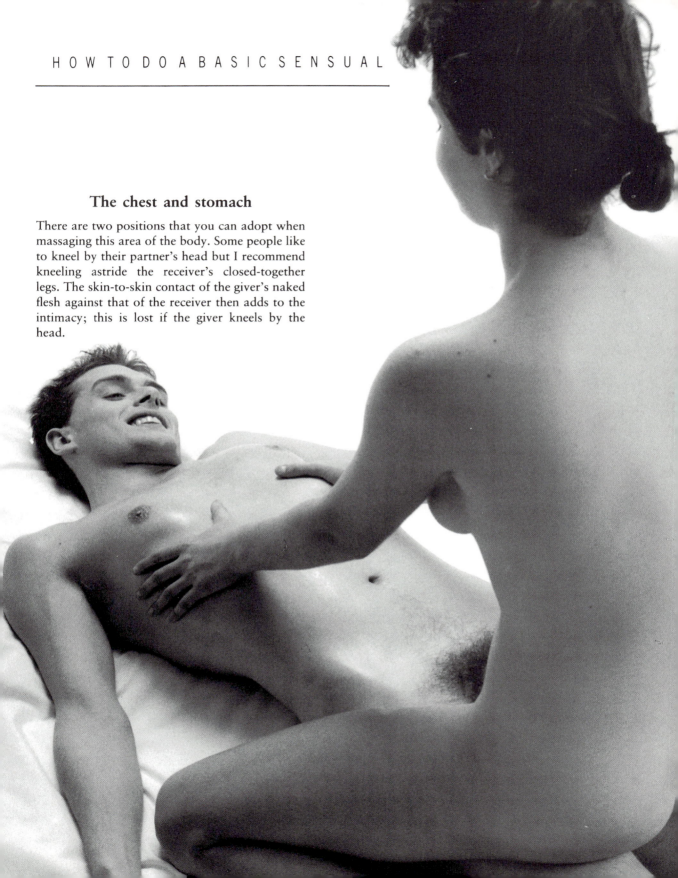

The chest and stomach

There are two positions that you can adopt when massaging this area of the body. Some people like to kneel by their partner's head but I recommend kneeling astride the receiver's closed-together legs. The skin-to-skin contact of the giver's naked flesh against that of the receiver then adds to the intimacy; this is lost if the giver kneels by the head.

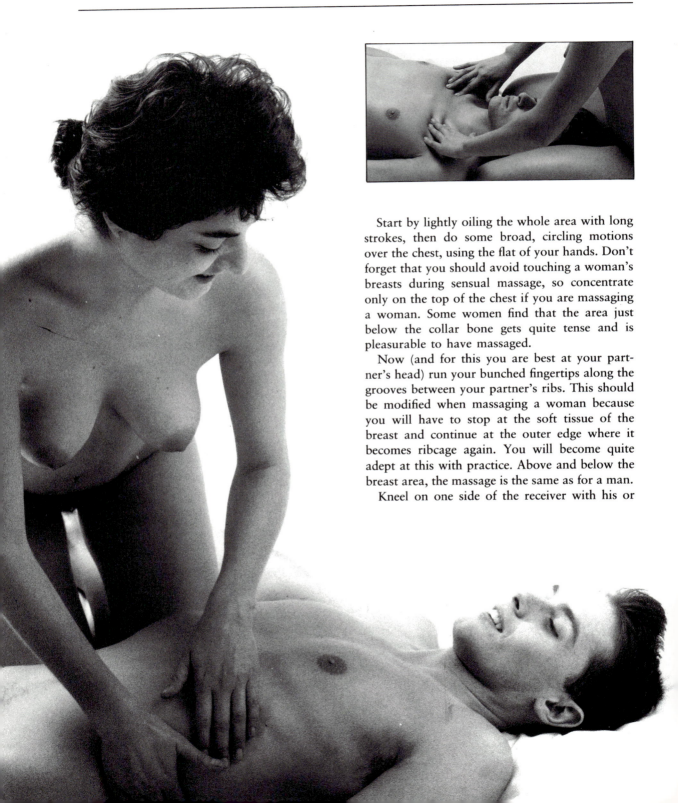

Start by lightly oiling the whole area with long strokes, then do some broad, circling motions over the chest, using the flat of your hands. Don't forget that you should avoid touching a woman's breasts during sensual massage, so concentrate only on the top of the chest if you are massaging a woman. Some women find that the area just below the collar bone gets quite tense and is pleasurable to have massaged.

Now (and for this you are best at your partner's head) run your bunched fingertips along the grooves between your partner's ribs. This should be modified when massaging a woman because you will have to stop at the soft tissue of the breast and continue at the outer edge where it becomes ribcage again. You will become quite adept at this with practice. Above and below the breast area, the massage is the same as for a man.

Kneel on one side of the receiver with his or

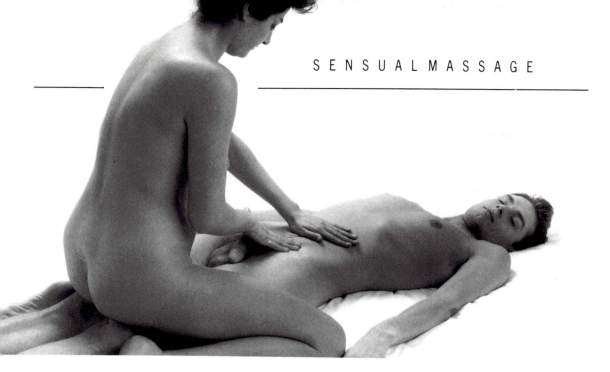

her arm on the opposite side stretched out at right angles to the body. Now, with plenty of oil on your hands, reach over and – working with pulling movements (see page 26) – bring your hands upwards from where the body meets the floor right up and over towards you, as far as the midline of the body. Do this using your hands alternately in a motion that takes them slightly farther down along the body at each stroke and pull with each hand slightly overlapping the track of the previous one. Carry on in this way until you reach the knee. Repeat the whole process from armpit to knee several times. Then kneel on the opposite side of the receiver and repeat the process again several times, massaging the second side. This is an exceptionally pleasant technique for most people, some of whom claim that it feels as if several people were massaging them at the same time. The idea is to make it seem as if there were one continuous wave of touch going down the whole length of the receiver's side.

I find that many people do not like to have their stomach massaged. Obviously, anything that tickles is counter-productive but this can possibly be avoided if the giver keeps the strokes firm and purposeful.

Two forms of massage are pleasant for many people. The first is broad circling, using both hands at once and overlapping them as they pass one another. Start with one hand, palm down, just below the breastbone and the other just above the pubic hair. Move each hand round in a circle. The lower hand should move in complete circles while the other breaks contact as it crosses the first. From most people's experience the motion of both hands should be clockwise rather than anti-clockwise. This is because food residues in the colon, just below the skin and muscle, are forced along it by the contraction of its muscular walls in a clockwise direction. This seems to be the way that energy flows in the skin and muscle of the abdomen. In fact, without explaining this I have, in the past, experimented with counter-clockwise movements – only to have the receiver ask me to stop at once because it felt so unpleasant. Some people do prefer counter-clockwise movements but they are rare.

Another motion that I find people enjoy on the stomach is small, circular movements, again going around within a larger circle. Imagine one of those whirling rides at a fairground in which each car rotates while the platform itself also spins around at speed. Mimic this at slow speed and you will be able to induce some lovely sensations in your partner.

Finish by doing some integrating movements to unite the whole of the chest and stomach before going on to massage the fronts of the legs.

The fronts of the legs

This area is treated much as the back of the legs but with more caution when massaging the lower leg because the shin-bone is so near the surface that pressure here can cause real pain.

The best position for massaging this area is with you kneeling so that one of your partner's lower legs is between your knees. You could perhaps start off by kneeling between the feet, with the receiver's legs apart so that you can oil both legs at once. But as you work on one leg at a time you will eventually need to alter your position so that the leg being worked on lies between your knees.

Start with some long strokes from groin to ankle, each stroke covering a large area of skin with as broad a hand movement as you can manage. Either use both hands, with your fingers pointing up the leg and being drawn downwards in waves alternately, or cup your hands across

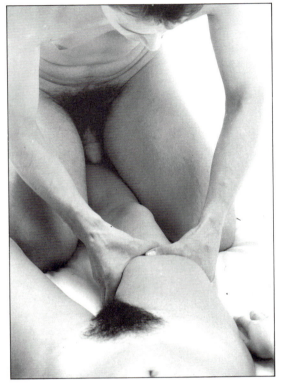

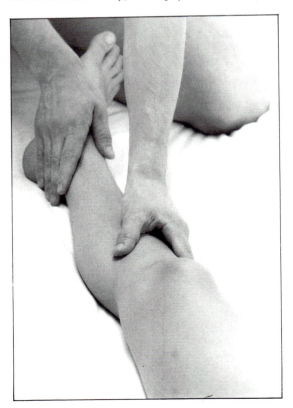

your partner's thigh or lower leg and move them alternately downwards in an overlapping pattern. Retrace this path but now with your hands more to the side of the leg. Then repeat it on the other side. In this way you will cover the whole leg in about three journeys. This can, of course, be repeated depending on what you have time for, and according to your partner's desires.

The thigh can be pleasantly massaged in two more ways. First, using your thumbs, work up from the knee to the groin, perhaps with the leg bent at the hip and the knee. See what feels best for you and your partner. 'Milk' the tissue, using your thumbs together, pushing in the same direction and gradually working up the thigh inch by inch until you reach the groin.

Secondly, massage the inside of the thigh and especially the 'tunnel' between the muscles from knee to groin. Some people like this to end with a massage of the groin area where the leg joins the stomach.

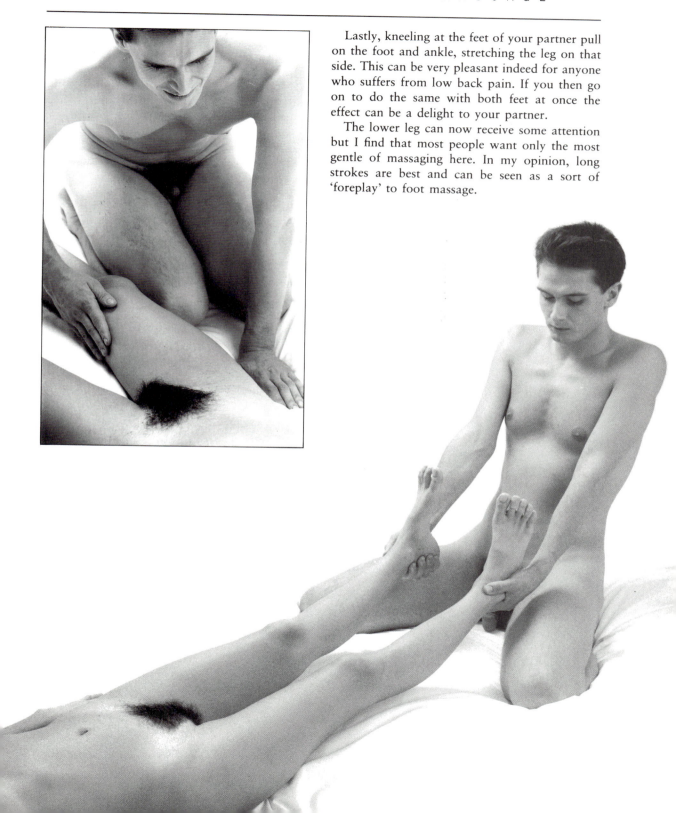

Lastly, kneeling at the feet of your partner pull on the foot and ankle, stretching the leg on that side. This can be very pleasant indeed for anyone who suffers from low back pain. If you then go on to do the same with both feet at once the effect can be a delight to your partner.

The lower leg can now receive some attention but I find that most people want only the most gentle of massaging here. In my opinion, long strokes are best and can be seen as a sort of 'foreplay' to foot massage.

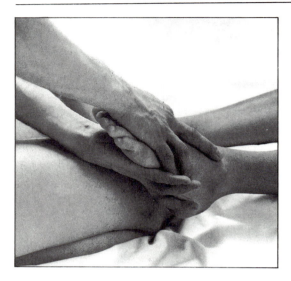

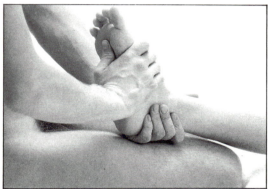

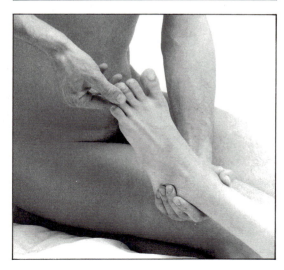

The feet

Like the hands, the feet can be very responsive, if massaged properly. Indeed I have known many women to say that they feel nearly orgasmic when their feet are massaged. In Chapter Five, we look at reflexology and what this specific kind of foot massage has to offer but here let us look at ordinary, sensual foot massage.

Many people who are ticklish become somewhat apprehensive at the very thought of having their feet *touched*, let alone *massaged* for any length of time. But this is a quite unwarranted fear, if the giver knows what he or she is about. When massaging the feet, always use firm, big-hand strokes. Start off by holding the foot between the flat of your hands and caressing it.

Now, gently but firmly pull the forefoot with one hand and, as this hand slides off the toes, grasp the foot again with the other hand and repeat the process. This sort of 'milking' movement provides quite exquisite sensations for most people. Repeat it several times, for each foot.

Now raise the foot with your hand and gently but firmly massage the sole just as you did the palm of the hand. Work around the area until you find the best places for the receiver, then concentrate on those. You will find that thumbs are best for this part of the foot massage. Do remember not to let your partner's foot simply fall back on to the floor. Set it down carefully before going on to the next foot.

Now pull the toes, one at a time, gently but firmly; this can be very pleasurable. Then run your fingertips through the spaces between the toes in order to massage the insides of the toes — as you did for the fingers.

Lastly, hold and massage the whole foot.

Finally – connection

Now you have completed all the separate areas of the body massage and your partner should be feeling very relaxed and may even have fallen asleep. End by connecting all the areas with some long, gentle strokes.

Sit or kneel at the side of the receiver and make long strokes with one hand up from one foot to the groin, across the lower stomach and down the other leg to the foot. Repeat this slowly and sensuously several times.

Now start just above the pubic area and run one hand up over the stomach and chest (around the breast) and down one arm, ending at the fingertips. Repeat this once more on this side and then do it twice more, but on the other side.

Finally, put one hand on your partner's fore-head and the other on his or her stomach above the pubic area and just below the navel – and just sit peacefully for a minute or so while you finally connect up the energy patterns you have been making during the massage.

Now your partner can open his or her eyes and you can take things from here. Most people find that they are so relaxed that they simply want to cuddle and go to sleep. This is especially likely if they have chosen to do the massage at the end of the day.

You may, of course, feel exceptionally loving and close and want to show this by going on to erotic massage which may, or may not, end in orgasm for one or both of you.

The important thing about sensual massage is that it is not generally a form of foreplay. I have said this to many couples who have come back a week or two later to say that they got carried away and ended up having sex. This is all very fine but, in the long term, it defeats the object. If sensual massage is to be a pleasurable activity *in itself* that does *not* have to end in sex then the receiver particularly has to be able to relax and feel totally at ease – trusting in the knowledge that there will be no price to pay at the end. Otherwise, much of this relaxation and trust is lost. I usually suggest that the partners agree not even to ask for sex on the first few occasions when they practise sensual massage. Once they see that the two can be separated and that a request for a massage does not have to end in sex, the two can be integrated as the weeks go by, perhaps using the further skills of erotic massage.

4

THE JOY OF EROTIC MASSAGE

In the last chapter, we saw that sensual massage is designed to
pleasure your partner without producing sexual arousal.

At first, many couples find this unlikely, but once they get used to the idea that they can give and receive physical pleasure without touching the genitals it alters their whole viewpoint – usually for the better.

What is erotic massage?

Erotic massage is, however, quite a different matter. Its aim is to arouse your partner as a prelude to sexual activity. The activity need not, of course, be full sexual intercourse. Some couples today, especially if they are not sure of one another's sexual past and are fearful of AIDS, use erotic massage as a prelude to foreplay that ends in mutual masturbation. This is nothing new, of course; couples have always done this, especially where they have been unsure of their contraceptive safety.

The massage routine is totally different then, when it comes to erotic massage. Now the whole idea is to use your body and hands to arouse your partner, rather than produce relaxation and sensuous feelings. We will consider here only those techniques that stop short of masturbation because this subject is well covered by other books.

If we are to have any hope of arousing a partner by using erotic massage we must understand what kinds of massage turn them on. In order to do this, it helps to be aware which areas of the body are particularly sensitive to erotic massage and which are not. As we have already seen, almost the whole body benefits from *sensual* massage.

The erogenous zones

The whole surface of our body is covered with nerve endings that transmit messages to the brain. But the whole body is not uniformly represented in the touch-sensitive areas of the brain; some areas have much more sensitivity than others. The mouth (especially the lips) and the fingertips, for example, are exceptionally well endowed with sensors and send messages to specific areas of the sensory brain.

While some areas are highly sensitive in relation to touch generally, others seem to have a specifically high erotic value ... so that when they are stimulated they create a feeling of sexual arousal. As with everything to do with human sexuality the variations are great – so do bear this in mind when giving your partner an erotic massage. Women, particularly, differ greatly in what they find erotic so a man will not necessarily be able to transfer experience learned from one woman to another.

Having said this, however, most people have in common some areas of their body that, when stimulated by the right person in the right way, cause them to become sexually aroused.

By and large, these areas are the 'forbidden zones' that we avoid when socially touching others. We avoid such contact because these areas are so sensitive that we could evoke inappropriate responses in those around us.

As a couple get to know one another the first erogenous zones to be discovered are the lips and the mouth. This takes us right back to babyhood when we experience so many pleasurable feelings through our mouth. A baby enjoys not only its mother's breast, its food, and its fingers, but also most of its toys, blankets, and a host of other things which it takes into its mouth as a highly efficient, early way of exploring them. The baby-like pleasures associated with oral love-making are highly enjoyable, relaxing and uninhibited and are thus of vital importance in erotic massage.

The next areas we discover are usually the face, ears and neck. These are anatomically close to the lips and mouth and are uncovered and therefore easily accessible when a couple are courting. Here again, the feelings evoked by contact with these areas take us back, however unconsciously, to our babyhood – when people kissed, stroked and patted our head. The head and neck area is therefore an excellent, non-threatening place at which to start an erotic massage.

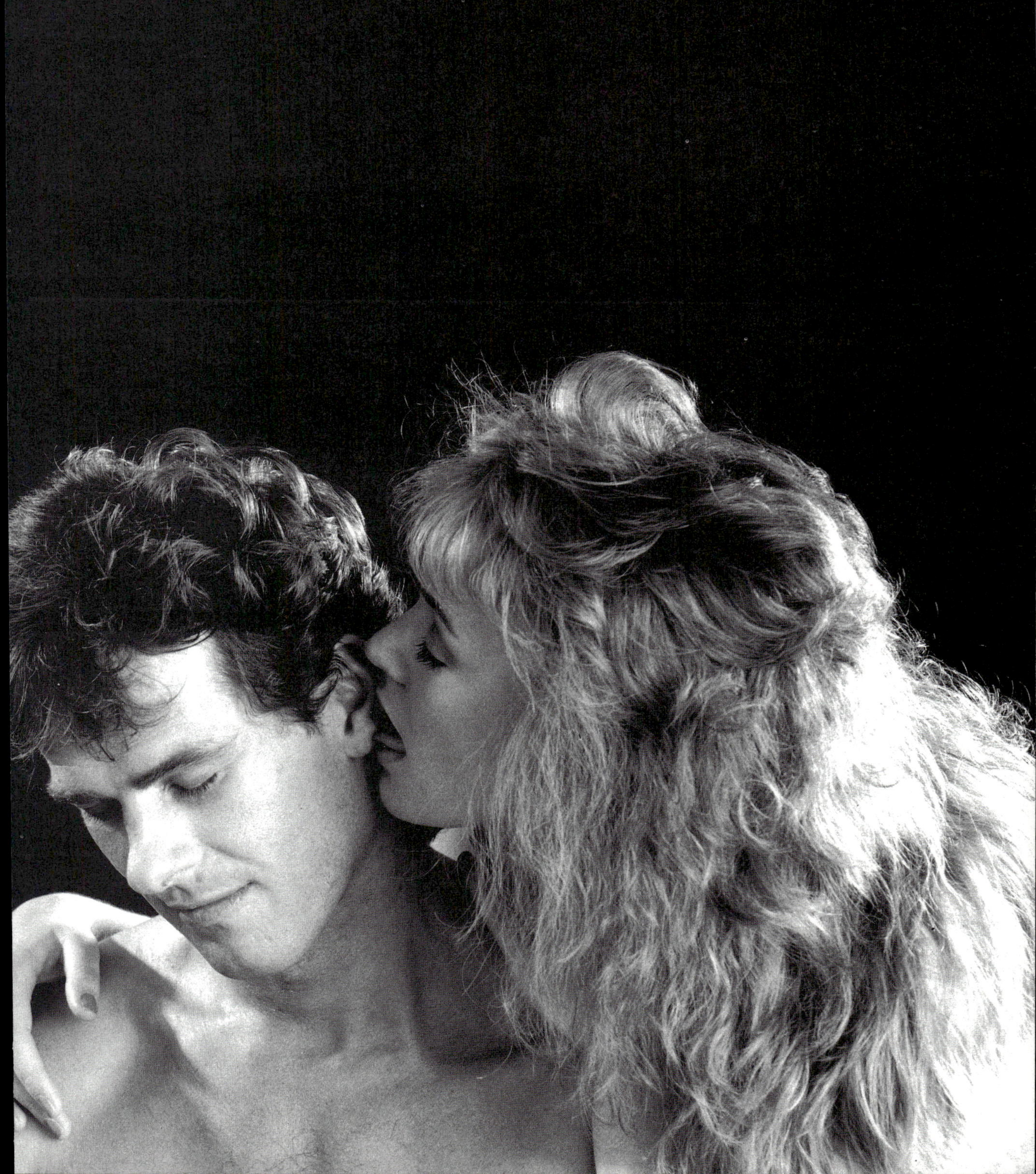

The inner surfaces of the thighs are sensitive, too, particularly in women. Indeed, some women become near-orgasmic when this area—perhaps in combination with the backs of their knees—is stroked or kissed.

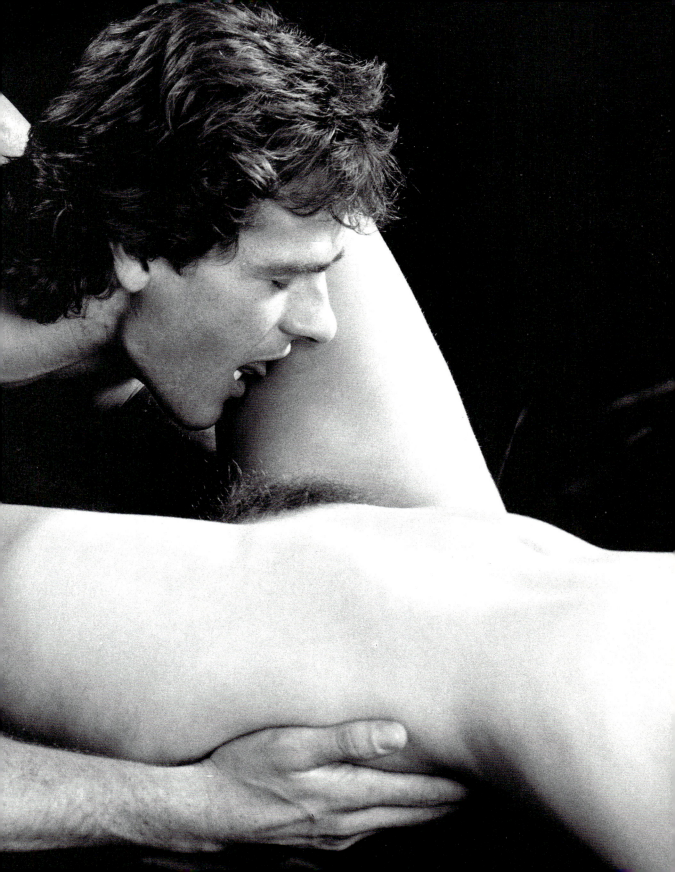

A woman's breasts can also be highly responsive of course, although about half of all women say that they are not as erotic as men imagine them to be. Far too many men straight away turn their attention to their partner's breasts and then wonder why she turns away. At least early on, while they are still becoming aroused, most women simply prefer to have their breasts gently

held and caressed. Later they might enjoy other things (see p. 91). This raises an important issue in relation to erotic massage: what feels good at one stage might well not at another, and *vice versa*. This makes erotic massage rather different from sensual massage in that the latter is much more predictable, partly because it does not rely on any emotional or sexual chemistry between the couple. Erotic massage, by definition, involves the intimate personalities of the couple *as lovers* and this means that the whole pursuit is more subject to the uniqueness of the individuals and to the state of their relationship at that time.

All of the anatomical areas so far discussed are known as the 'secondary erogenous zones'. The 'primary erogenous zones' are the penis, scrotum and perineal area in men and the equivalent area in women, which is called the vulva. We shall not be considering these in this book because there are many other publications that deal with stimulation of these areas.

Generally, women are more responsive to touch than are men. This is because they have more pleasure zones than men have. Women are also more at ease with their bodies and feel free to experience pleasure from them more readily than do most men. Boys are brought up to be tough and to deny their feelings and consequently many men find it hard to relax and even to acknowledge their pleasurable sensations, unless, of course, they are genital. Men come to believe that the only 'real' sexual activity they should indulge in and enjoy is genital activity and that anything else is a waste of time, or 'feminine'.

For these reasons, while most women greatly enjoy erotic massage that excludes the genitals men are eager, or even frankly impatient, to get on with 'the real thing'. This would be no tragedy in itself if men married men but they do not. Many women complain that their partners lack sensitivity and patience – going straight for the genitals as if nothing else mattered.

This is perhaps not too surprising, given the way boys are reared to be 'men' in our culture, but it is also encouraged by the fact that for most men their best erotic sensations occur in the area covered by their swimming trunks. This is not so for women.

The illustrations on the previous page show the erogenous zones in men and women and it can be seen at a glance that women have a much greater area over which they enjoy being stimulated. In fact, some women can be brought to orgasm by the stimulation of almost any part of their anatomy. This certainly could not be said of men.

While almost any part of the body can be touched, stroked, massaged or kissed during an erotic massage, for best effect it makes sense to concentrate on those areas of your partner's body that you have found from experience to be erogenous. Having said this, men often need encouragement and 'tuition' if they are really to enjoy being massaged erotically. They assume that their erogenous zones are few in number – and well-known to them – and so miss out on many others that could be developed with practice. But a woman who is enthusiastic, willing and inventive will find ways to delight her partner, however un-erotic he thinks himself to be at the start.

Some basic skills

Let us now look at some basic techniques for lovers to use when doing an erotic massage, just as we did when looking at sensual massage. Here, as then, it is important to remember that these are only suggestions and that you will find your own special methods as you become more adventurous and skilled.

At first, most people think of erotic massage as involving only manual skills but it can include far, far more as we shall see. Whatever technique you use, the thing to remember is that the slower you go and the more you tease the better the effects you will achieve. Erotic massage has nothing in common with quickie sex – delicious though that might be at the right time. Erotic massage techniques prolong love-making by means of erotic touch until both of you are so crazy with passion for one another that you cannot bear to delay intercourse for a second longer.

Here then, are some basic techniques and skills that are worth trying and practising.

USE YOUR HANDS

Erotic massage is very different from the sensual variety because here the sole purpose is to arouse your partner and there are no holds barred. No longer do you have to stifle your natural desire to become intensely involved because your intimate involvement is the key to success.

In the next section, we shall look at each area of the body and how to massage it specifically for the greatest erotic effect but here let us look at some of the basic strokes.

Gliding is particularly erotic. Run your hands over large areas of your partner's body, especially the back, chest and breasts, buttocks and spine. It is not necessary to oil your partner for this but if you have just completed a sensual massage he or she will already be slightly lubricated. Make the strokes long and integrating rather than short and jerky. Start by letting your hands 'float' over the surface of the receiver's body and when breaking the stroke do so gently and sensitively.

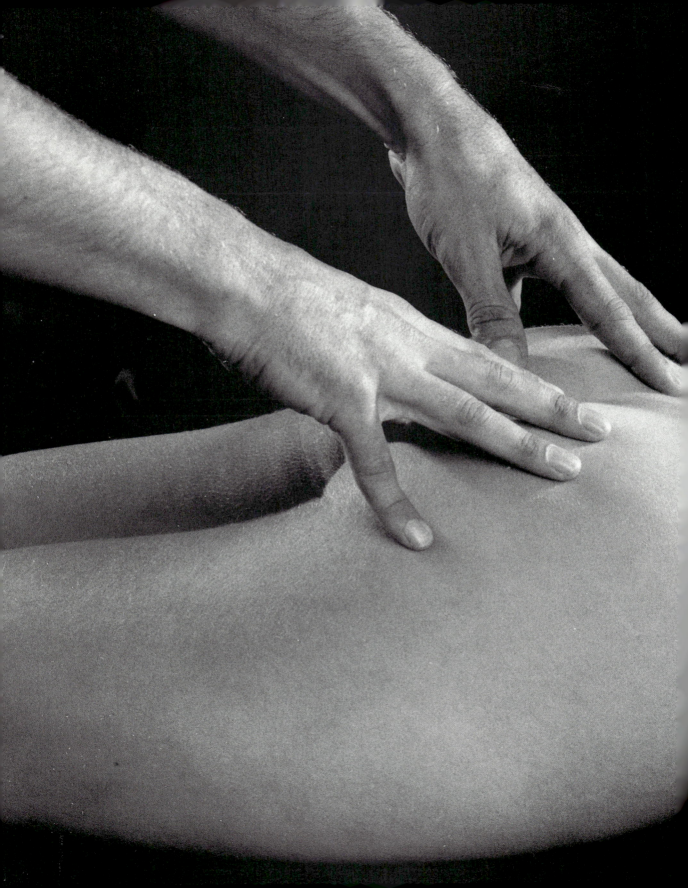

Kneading and other semi-deep strokes can be very erotic in the right places. Some people find that, once they begin to become aroused, areas of tension such as the top of the back around the shoulders and the base of the neck can be exquisitely erotic if the amount of pressure applied is just right. By and large, though, deep and semi-deep strokes are best reserved for your sensual massage.

Light touching, using your fingers as lightly as if they were spider's legs, is highly arousing. Let your hands wander all over your partner's body just touching the skin's surface with your fingertips in a teasing, not tickling, way. Explore further wherever it makes them shudder with

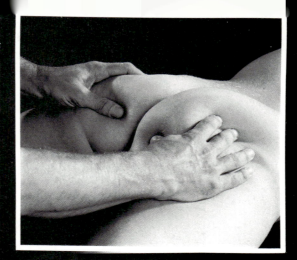

delight. Almost anywhere is good to try. Trace long paths linking areas that you learn are responsive. We are avoiding the genital area for the purposes of this book but just a warning here that these spider's legs strokes are too ticklish for most people's genitals.

Walking your fingertips around various sensitive parts can be a delight and gentle *pinching and squeezing* can be good, if done in the right places—that is, the fleshy parts of the body.

As your partner becomes highly aroused he or she might enjoy actually being squeezed hard. This is true of some women's breasts and indeed some men's nipples. Many people like to have their buttocks squeezed and, of course, a whole body hug can make you feel very close indeed. Some couples who become very close emotionally during their erotic massage say that they occasionally feel that they want their bodies to merge into one another, so deep is the intimacy that they feel.

Smacking is a rather specialised form of stroke but one which is enjoyed by some. Indeed, there are women who need to be smacked, playfully, before they can truly enjoy the sex that is to follow. This is probably because they are unconsciously guilty about enjoying, or even wanting, sex and feel that they should be punished in advance for being so 'naughty'. It is a foolish lover who does not include such play if it turns his partner on.

Of course you don't have to limit yourself to using your hands to massage your partner's body where he or she best enjoys intimate contact. At first this might feel a little strange but as you become used to it you will become very skilled and give your partner sensations that he or she never knew were possible.

In fact, a fun game to play is to forbid the use of hands altogether and see how inventive, erotic, and sensual you can be without their help.

Remember that whatever you do, and however you achieve it, the only goal is to give your partner the best erotic sensations and to drive him or her to higher levels of passion.

USE YOUR HAIR

A very erotic thing for a woman to do is to let her hair trail over various sensitive areas of the man's body. A man can do this too if his hair is long enough. The gentle, teasing nature of this form of 'massage' is hard to beat.

USE YOUR MOUTH

Obviously you will want to kiss your partner's erogenous zones but there are many other mouth games you can play, too. Run your tongue around sensitive areas in a teasing but non-tickling way; give your partner little nibbles and nips with your teeth – but taking care not to hurt him or her. Blow puffs of air over highly sensitive areas. Suck an area of skin into your mouth and work your tongue on it. The combinations are endless.

Some couples enjoy using their tongues to 'bathe' one another. Make sure that your tongue is wet with saliva, then run it all over areas of your partner's body as if you were washing it with your tongue. Blowing dry air over these wetted areas can be exquisite for the receiver.

As a part of this tongue bath, or maybe separately, don't forget to kiss your partner's body really erotically. Kissing the palm of the hand, for example, can be very sensual; kiss the fingers too and perhaps take them into your mouth one at a time. In other words, extend your ideas of kissing from simply planting your lips on your partner's skin to becoming a way of oral love-making in every sense of the word. Oral sex has come to be seen as a very narrow business involving one partner kissing or sucking the genitals of the other but this misses out a whole range of wonderful sensations, many of which are highly erotic.

THE ART OF EROTIC MASSAGE

IF YOU ARE A WOMAN, USE YOUR BREASTS

Either ask your partner to oil your breasts or, alternatively, smooth a little oil over the area of his body you intend to massage and then use your breasts to massage him there. This drives most men wild and often has a similar effect on the woman. Using your breasts to massage his nipples can be especially erotic.

In addition to this extensive repertoire you could also go back to any of the strokes or techniques that you found produced erotic effects when doing your sensual massage. Instead of reducing the erotic effect as you did then the idea now is to enhance it.

USE YOUR MIND

The mind is our most powerful sex organ and the skin is the largest, so between the two, it is easy to see that erotic massage is a very powerful and arousing pastime, involving them both.

Really concentrate on your partner. Your practice with the sensual massage will come in handy here. Don't work out the shopping list or let worries about the mortgage clutter your mind — lose yourself in the present activity and give your partner the best sensations you can. He or she will be doing the same for you so, if you have built up some tension and expectation as a result of your sensual massage, now is the time to defuse it.

THE ART OF EROTIC MASSAGE

USE TOYS AND AIDS

Electrical massagers, feathers, furs, ice, silk, leather, rubber, and a host of other material aids can be used to enhance the erotic quality of the massage. It's fun experimenting with these in order to increase your repertoire and enjoyment.

Setting the scene

How you set the scene for erotic massage depends somewhat on whether or not it is to be a follow-on from sensual massage.

If you are following on from sensual massage then you will already have made your environment conducive to relaxation and not being disturbed. The only difference now perhaps is that you might want to go to the bed rather than stay on the massage mat or floor. You will by now be intent on more uninhibited sharing and the firmness of the floor will probably be uncomfortable for cuddling and anything that follows.

However, if you are starting out to give one another an erotic massage without these preliminaries then look back to page 16 to see which of the preparations listed there and on the following pages apply to your plans for an erotic encounter. Some things will be more important to get right and others less so. For example, privacy, while important when massaging each other sensually is vital when doing erotic massage. Few people can become sufficiently uninhibited to really enjoy themselves erotically if they fear interruption.

Some couples like to enhance the mood of the room for erotic occasions, perhaps by putting on some music that has a special romantic or erotic significance for them.

Clothes, while definitely *not* a part of sensual massage, can play an important role in erotic massage. Many men enjoy their partner being dressed up in a special dress or underwear and some women obtain pleasure from their man dressing in particular ways. Undressing then becomes an integral part of the massage and one part of the body can be revealed at a time and worked on as a prolonged tease – leaving the most responsive areas until last, of course.

Jewellery, frankly a nuisance during sensual massage, is now quite acceptable – provided that it does not get in the way. An ankle or waist chain, for example, can look very sexy and highly arousing in itself, especially against a tanned skin. Perfume also adds to the erotic atmosphere.

How you prepare your body and that of your partner is also more important than for sensual massage. Bathing or showering together is a good start . . . in fact it is nice to begin the massage in a shared shower or bath.

Mental preparation is just as important as it is for sensual massage except that now, instead of stilling your mind and focusing on your partner's pleasure, you excite your mind, perhaps by fantasizing a favourite scene. Some couples further enhance this by sexy talk.

All of this preparation raises the level of sexual expectation and tension and extends the amount of time and pleasure you will derive from the massage itself. In a rush-and-hurry world in which many couples hurry through their 'love-making' as if it were a meal in a fast-food restaurant, this leisurely approach pays dividends and can even completely revive a flagging sex life.

Couples often ask me whether or not they *should* do a sensual massage before starting on their erotic massage. Frankly there's no simple answer to this because some people find that they usually end up making love after they have massaged one another sensually and others never do. Obviously, erotic massage is sufficient in itself and does not have to follow or be a part of a sensual massage. I still think it is valuable to separate the two pursuits on most occasions so that the person asking for a massage doesn't have to expect to pay for it by having to go on to sex if they do not want to do so. Obviously, this is not a problem when it comes to erotic massage because sex is intended from the start.

The main thing that most couples who practise both these techniques find is that they become much more honest with one another about what they really want. Too often a man who feels in need of a cuddle or a back rub after a long drive home from work thinks he has to clothe his request in some sort of sexual language or his partner will think him a wimp. He therefore asks for sex when really he wants something else. Because his heart (and his penis) are not in it he is more prone to failure and this, added to the fact that it wasn't really sex that he wanted in the first place, leads to disappointments, failures, rows, bitterness, and even perhaps to an extra-marital search by one or both partners to vent their frustration.

If as a result of asking for what they want, and being sure that they will receive it, a couple becomes more open about what it is that they *do* want, then massaging one another greatly enhances the relationship. Women too, often find it difficult to be honest; it is not just a problem that men have. Sometimes a woman goes along with sex when she really would rather not, but had she offered her man a sensual massage or even a stimulating erotic one followed by masturbation both would be happy and she would not end up feeling put upon.

Some couples do deals with one another in this sphere of their lives and who is to say that they are wrong? For example, the woman may be feeling sexy but the man may be too tired for intercourse. Or he may have had a recent failure and be wary of things going wrong again. Such a man might, however, be happy to settle for an erotic massage, with or without masturbation. It is non-threatening and because his partner is being so uninhibitedly arousing to him (and probably to herself, too) he doesn't feel so bad about 'letting her down' by not having sex.

The permutations and combinations of sensual massage, erotic massage, masturbation, and intercourse are numerous and any thoughtful couple who want to please one another will work out a plan that suits them on any particular occasion. With flexibility and good will on both sides there are few sexual and intimate situations that cannot be dealt with lovingly, using a combination of sensual and erotic massage.

Erotic things to do

Any couple prepared to be adventurous will discover for themselves what they best enjoy but here I list a few of the things that many couples have found to work. This list is just a start; an uninhibited couple will easily be able to double it over some months of pleasuring one another.

HAIR AND SCALP

Massage your partner's scalp and head, especially over tense muscles at the temples or at the back of the head. This can be a good soothing start because it is so relaxing. As we saw on page 60 the head and neck are also easily accessible (because they are not covered by clothes) and are areas of the body we are used to having petted from very early in life. This makes them a soothing, non-threatening place at which to begin.

● Nuzzle your face into the hair and run your fingers through it repeatedly as you stroke your partner's scalp.

● Some women enjoy having a little perfume massaged into their scalp.

● Kiss one another's hair.

● Some people like to have their hair brushed by their partner in a rhythmical and sensual way. This can be very erotic in the right setting.

FACE AND EARS

Kiss your partner's face all over and hold it in your hands, gently and lovingly.

● Plant masses of tiny and light kisses on various parts of the face, especially on the eyelids, and the ears.

● Touch the inside of the ear lobe, very lightly and sensuously, and trace paths around the outside too.

● Brush the lobe of the ear with a fingertip and gently bite it. Massage the ear with your tongue.

● Now gently run a fingertip over the eyelids; touch the lips; make tiny circles over the cheeks; and so on.

● Kiss one another on the lips and mouth using all the erotic skills you have learned during your time together.

NECK

Stroke the sides of the neck with several finger-tips bunched together.

● Breathe on to your partner's neck so that he or she feels the gentle warmth of your breath.

● Run your hands under the hair line and stroke the back of the neck with your fingertips.

● Bring your hands round to the front and gently trace a path along the collarbone.

● Plant kisses on your partner's throat, working from the top of the breastbone up to the tip of the chin. Repeat this up and down several times.

CHEST AND BREASTS

For him Circle his nipples with your tongue and give them gentle, teasing bites. Stroke his chest all over, perhaps with some sensuous material such as silk. Rub your body over his chest, perhaps massaging his chest with your breasts through the silk.

Experiment until you discover what drives him wild. This may take some time because most men have little or no experience of what they best like done to this area of their bodies.

For her This is not so for women, many of whom play with their breasts when masturbating and are thus quite expert on the subject of what turns them on. A sensible man watches his partner masturbate so that he knows exactly what she best likes and how she does it.

THE ART OF EROTIC MASSAGE

● Use the palm of your hand to brush lightly over her breasts (use some oil if you both want to massage her properly). Apply the oil all over the breasts and the top of her chest. Apply it slowly and teasingly leaving the nipples until last.

● Gently rub the nipples between your fingers. Squeeze them if this is what she likes. Push them into the breast itself and massage them in this position. Gently pull the nipples, perhaps slightly twisting them at the same time.

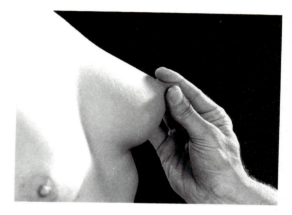

● Take as much of the breast into your mouth as you can and suck hard. Apply various kinds of suction to the nipples, at the same time tonguing them. When playing with one breast in this way, be sure to stroke the other one at the same time.

● Wet her nipples with saliva and blow softly on them.

● Grasp both breasts at once and gently rub them together.

● Cover her breasts with some pleasant food-stuff or drink and lick it off.

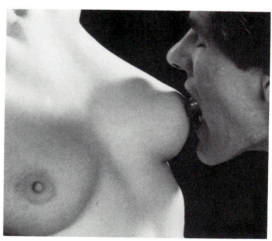

● Flutter your eyelashes over her nipples or use a feather. Rub her breasts with a fur glove.

● Rub your nipples against hers.

● Massage her breasts with your feet.

STOMACH

Use a sensuous material to stroke your partner's stomach. Silk underwear or stockings, especially if she has just taken them off, can be a really erotic experience. Kiss the whole of the stomach right down to the pubic hair but teasingly refrain from actually touching it.

● Put your tongue into the navel and rotate it. Now blow into the navel.

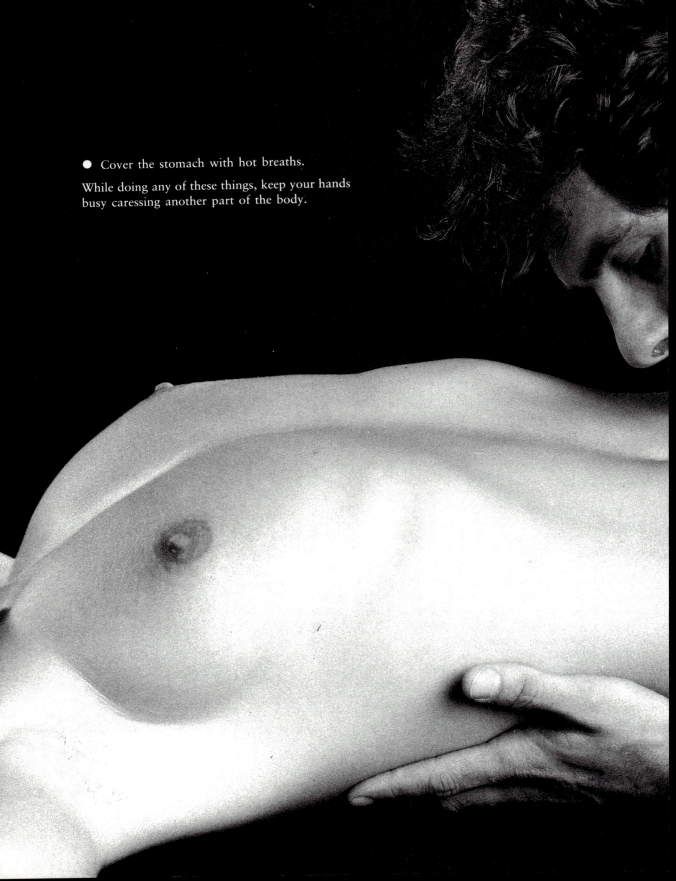

● Cover the stomach with hot breaths.

While doing any of these things, keep your hands busy caressing another part of the body.

ARMS AND HANDS

Perhaps using a little more oil, massage the arms with long, sensuous strokes. This will temporarily reduce the erotic temperature a little, which all adds to the tension and anticipation.

Now take your partner's fingers and massage them gently and slowly.

● Put one finger at a time into your mouth and suck and kiss it.

● Explore the palm of the hand with your tongue, probing it deeply.

● Tongue the areas between the fingers.

● Carry over any skills learned from your sensual massage that you found your partner really enjoyed.

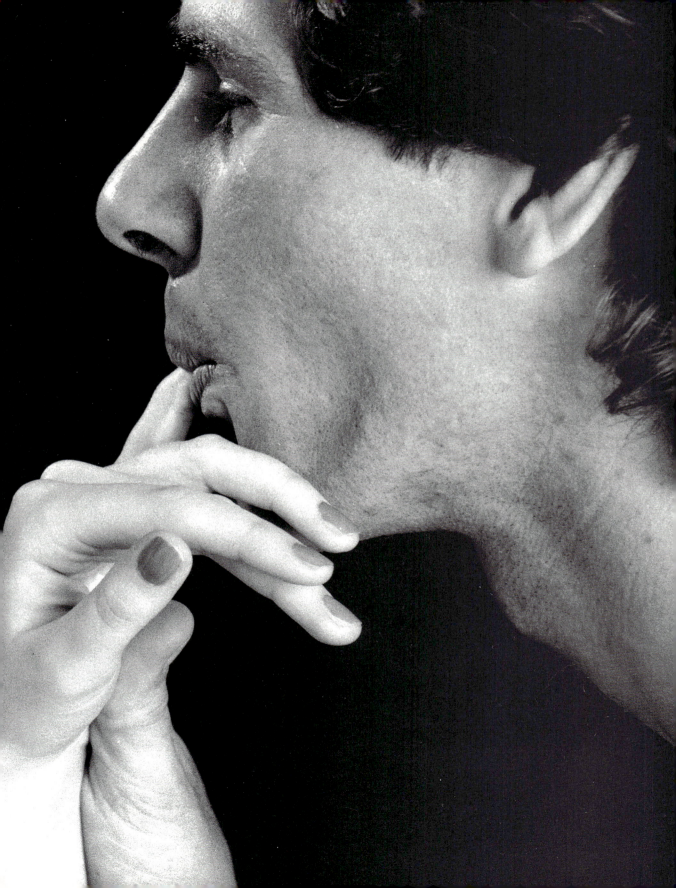

BACK

Roll your partner over lovingly and massage his or her back with some oil using large, broad, gliding strokes. Find those tense areas at the top of the shoulders and lower neck and soothe away the knots. Do this while sitting astride your partner's body so that you grip him or her between your thighs, with your pubic hair and genital areas sliding over the buttocks and lower back whenever you move around to reach the highest parts of the back and neck.

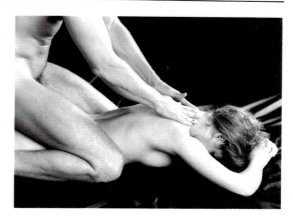

● Do some long gliding strokes up and down the large muscles at the sides of the spine, using your fingertips bunched together. Lose no opportunity to ensure the largest amount of skin contact between yourself and your partner.

Now lower your body position somewhat to get ready to do the buttocks. Sit between your partner's open legs as he or she lies on the front. This opens up the genital area and is in itself highly erotic.

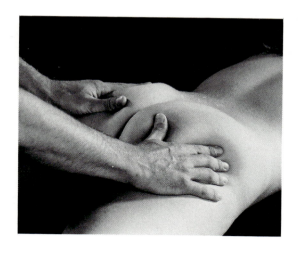

BUTTOCKS

Many people greatly enjoy having their buttocks massaged and erotically stroked.

● Massage the buttocks and end up with teasing strokes down the crack between them.

● If your partner likes it, continue this stroke down to the anus and circle it in a teasing way.

● Massage the area between the anus and the vaginal opening or the base of the penis. This area – the perineum – is highly erogenous for most people yet is often totally ignored even by quite experienced couples.

● Do some long strokes from high up on the top of the spine – perhaps with your tongue – and continue on right down between the buttocks and then down to the anus or perineum. Make this journey long and highly erotic. Also be sure to make the endpoint worth waiting for.

● Massage the innermost parts of the buttocks but avoid the anus. Kiss the buttocks and run your hair all over them.

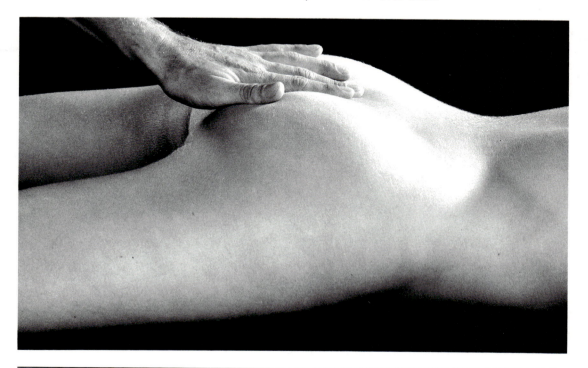

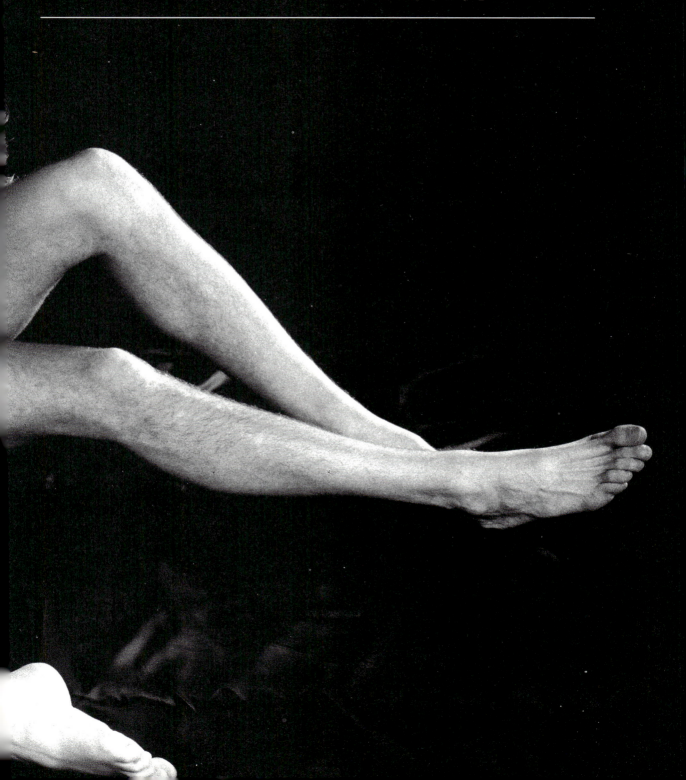

LEGS AND FEET

Because the massage described so far has become so erotic the time has now come to slow the pace down a little:

● Smooth some oil on to your partner's legs and massage them, using long, gliding strokes from buttocks to ankles. Remember, as with the sensual massage, to put very little pressure on the skin as you go down and to be quite firm as you push up.

● The inner parts of the thighs are especially erotic for women, as are the areas behind the knees. Spend a lot of time massaging these areas and cover them with kisses and licks.

● Run your tongue right up to the pubic hair but do not actually touch it. Start behind the knee and with your tongue trace a path up to the genitals, via the inner thighs. Go back down again with your tongue and then cross to the other leg and repeat the process until he or she can bear it no more.

● Massage the feet as in the sensual massage section but this time use your mouth to kiss and enclose the toes and massage the feet themselves with parts of your body, including your genitals.

● Take your partner's foot and use it as if it were a massager to caress parts of your body you would like massaged and stroked.

WHOLE BODY

Lastly, as with the sensual massage, but for different reasons, use your whole body to integrate all the areas you have been massaging so far. Rub yourself up and down various parts of his or her body, now using your genitals as additional massage aids. Go for long gliding strokes, first with you and then with your partner on top. Use various parts of your partner to massage yourself and generally luxuriate in the feel and warmth of one another's bodies.

By now you should be highly aroused and ready to start on more specifically genital play. How you do this is up to you and is beyond the scope of this book. Most couples who have taken their erotic massage this far will be so highly aroused that almost any genital activity will be exciting and orgasms should be rich, full and deeply satisfying.

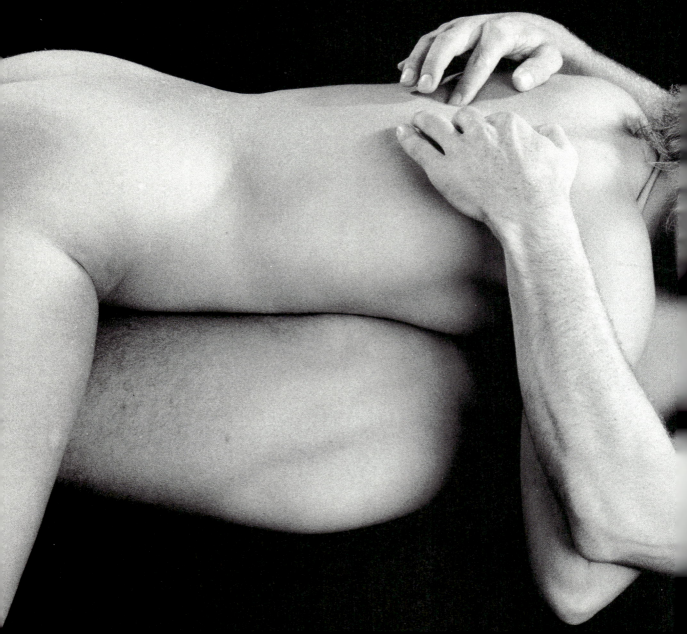

5

NATURAL THERAPIES, MASSAGE AND SEX

Although sex has many negative overtones in Western, Judaeo-Christian culture,
this is not so around the world and probably never has been.

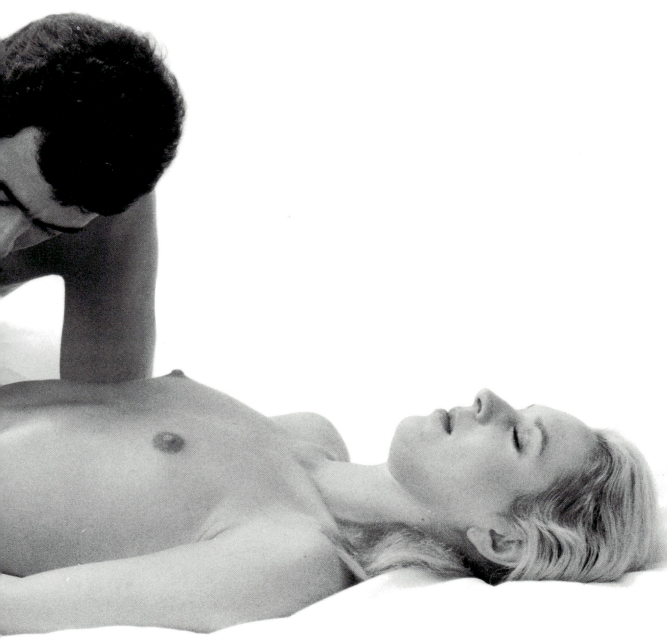

True, there have always been some prohibitions on sex (there are no cultures where anything goes with anybody at any time) but in the West we seem to have segregated sex and made it guilt-ridden, something we don't talk about—or even something we wish would go away.

Elsewhere in the world, on the contrary, sex is seen as an integral part of the splendour of life, and central to it. The ancient orientals placed sex on a high plane both in the universal scheme of things and for the individual. For them it fulfilled all kinds of spiritual roles as well as biological ones. Sadly, nowadays, the Western view of sexuality is fast taking over.

In my view this is a pity because sex is indeed a spiritual affair and the union between a couple who are lovers goes way beyond the physical embrace. Those readers who have this kind of relationship will know exactly what I mean.

In an increasingly harsh and godless world, I believe that for many the only glimpse of the spiritual world is to be found in their one-to-one relationship. In the absence of anything else, this is surely no bad thing.

What I perceive professionally is perfectly in keeping with this. As a marital therapist I see couples who function very well on the physical plane but certainly do not do so at the spiritual level. Their relationship is impoverished as a result, and they know it but do not know why.

All of this rather high-flown thinking becomes important when looking beyond the actual physical contact of sensual and erotic massage to the natural therapies, many of which are based on a wider understanding of the world than is the case in Western medicine. Indeed, the vast majority of such therapies have a vitally important spiritual dimension at their heart.

In this chapter I am looking very briefly at what some of the natural and often ancient massage therapies have to offer today's Western couple. While most readers will almost certainly use the sensual and erotic massage sections of the book on a day-to-day basis there are, I hope, some pleasant, relaxing and stimulating techniques in this chapter that could enrich almost any couple's experience. Few of us will be able to—

or, indeed, even want to—embrace the philosophy or way of life that accompanies some of the therapies discussed but we can take from them techniques and skills that will help us to improve our sensual and erotic lives.

Let us start by looking at a relatively simple form of natural therapy that any couple can benefit from—aromatherapy.

Aromatherapy

This is an ancient art, dating back at least to the Pharaohs of Egypt, in which essential oils from plants are used medically to cure physical ailments or for their effects on the mind and the emotions. Occasionally the oils are taken internally but most often they are massaged into the skin, through which they are readily absorbed, especially if applied to skin which is warm after a bath.

As the oils are extracted from plants and flowers they can be expensive but a little goes a long way as they are very potent. The very best oils are available from major department stores or by mail order from the Marguerite Maury Clinic, Park Lane Hotel, London W1Y 8BX, but many high-street chains now stock medium-priced versions that are ideal for massage.

Aromatherapy is easy to practise at home because all you need is the oil and your hands. We shall not consider the therapeutic use of aromatherapy oils here because this is something that should be done only by a professional, but we shall look at their use as part of sensual and erotic massage. In this context the best way to choose which oil to use is to see which scent you prefer.

If you like the smell of a particular oil, it will probably have a relaxing effect on you as its 'odoriferous molecules'—that is, the active ingredients that create the smell—act on your brain via your nostrils. Smell is a very primitive and highly developed sensory system in all animals, and humans are no exception.

Once you have bought your oil it can be used a

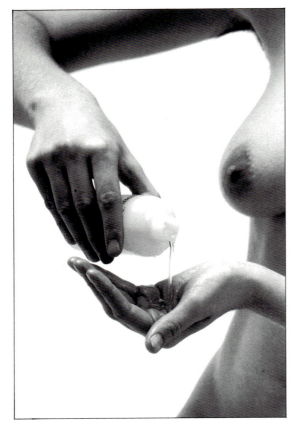

few drops at a time in the bath. You can also put three or four drops into a bowl of hot water to inhale; or you can use it to massage yourself or your partner.

Unless you have bought an aromatherapy oil that is ready for use straight from the bottle, it is cheaper and perfectly effective to dilute it with a carrier oil such as soya or almond oil; use three or four drops of oil to one eggcupful of the carrier oil.

To enhance the effects of the oil, the receiver's skin should first be warmed either by massaging him or her without oil or by using it after he or she has had a bath or shower. Use the oil to massage your partner as discussed throughout the book. The difference between using ordinary massage oil and aromatherapy oils is that the exquisite scent of the latter will have effects of its own which will add to the relaxing or erotic effects of the massage itself.

Here are a few notes on particular aromatherapy oils and their uses in conditions that might be of interest to you as you learn to use these oils as part of your sensual and erotic life together.

Rosemary oil is said to have an aphrodisiac effect. Add four drops to an eggcupful of soya oil, mix well and massage into the area around the base of the spine.

Caraway oil added to the bath has been found to help ease period pains.

Sage oil, 3 drops to a bowl of warm water or bidet and splashed up into the vagina helps cure infections and soothe irritations.

Peppermint can be used as a gargle, in a dose of 2 drops to a cup or glassful of warm water. This is repeated when necessary as a cure for unpleasant-smelling breath.

Using aromatherapy oils is unlikely to become a regular part of your massage routine on the grounds of cost but for those special occasions when you want to enhance the mood or feel particularly relaxed, they can be quite magical.

Shiatsu

This literally means 'finger pressure' and is an ancient Japanese art. It is different from Western forms of massage in that it uses only pressure and stretching strokes. There are no kneading, friction, or gliding ones.

The practitioner of Shiatsu uses fingers, elbows, knees or feet to work on the many acupuncture points along the body's energy channels. It is rather like the closely-related art of Chinese acupressure but this latter uses only fingers to apply pressure.

Although much of Western massage is in fact aimed at balancing the body's energy patterns and flows, we do not usually talk of things in this way, whereas Shiatsu confronts this head-on, as its main aim. Indeed, a professional practitioner works on the 'patient' in a way designed to balance body, mind, spirit, emotions, and so on, even if the 'patient' originally went for help with an 'illness'.

Shiatsu is becoming increasingly popular in the West as a treatment for problems as different as stress, childbirth pains, and everyday ailments.

As you would imagine, it is a lifetime's task to become truly expert at Shiatsu but there is much that the amateur can achieve at home with a little practice. As with all the forms of massage I have discussed, the results largely depend on the level of communication between the giver and the receiver.

Posture is important when practising Shiatsu. Both giver and receiver should be relaxed and when you apply the pressure to an acupuncture point it should all come from the area just below your navel (the *hara*) rather than from your arms or shoulders. It is also important to press on the pressure points (*tsubos*) with your thumb or palm at right angles to your body.

Kneel with your legs slightly apart so that you feel steady and firm. This will enable you to sustain the pressure over some time without losing your balance or becoming tired. Keep your arms straight. Ideally, the receiver should be on the floor, but if the relevant *tsubos* can be easily reached with the receiver sitting in a chair, that is fine.

Although the true professional uses many parts of his body to apply pressure, it is easiest for the beginner to start with his or her thumbs. Apply pressure with one thumb only, though at times both will need to be used, one on top of the other. Use the pad of your thumb and allow the rest of your hand to lie on the receiver's body to maintain contact. In fact, always keep your hands in contact with your partner's body; if necessary use one hand to apply the pressure and allow the other to rest on the body close to your working hand.

You can also use your palm to press over the person's *hara*; press with your arm at right angles to the receiver's body.

Pressure during a shiatsu massage usually feels pleasant and comfortable to the receiver but if ever he or she feels pain or discomfort, stop, because this may suggest internal problems.

The receiver need not be naked for this type of massage but it is probably better if he or she is.

Before describing a brief massage sequence that can be used by anyone who has some experience of sensual massage as described in the early parts of the book, it makes sense to think for a moment about times when it is unwise to do such a massage.

● Beware especially of varicose veins.

● Avoid the abdomen of a pregnant woman and, in later stages of pregnancy, avoid pressure on the legs.

● Do not massage anyone who is exhausted.

● If your partner has a fever do not massage him or her.

● Do not massage anyone with a contagious skin disease, a slipped disc, or broken bones.

● Do not massage anyone who is on steroid drugs (such as cortisone).

Anyone who really wants to learn about performing a good shiatsu massage must read a thorough book that details exactly what to do. Here, though, is a brief résumé of a simple shiatsu massage that will integrate your partner's energy systems and enhance his or her sense of well-being. Remember that all of these strokes act on various acupuncture points in such a way as to alter and to normalise energy flows in them.

✳ Ask your partner to lie on his or her stomach, flat on the floor or mat. Place your hands diagonally across the back, over one shoulder blade and the opposite hip and stretch the spine as the receiver breathes out. Change over your hands and repeat the stretch but the other way round, so as to stretch the spine across the other dimension of the back.

✳ Press along the top of each shoulder and rotate the shoulder blades. Here there are meridians (energy flow channels) that have to do with tension and stress. These call for attention in most of us and especially in those who have a tendency to nervousness and tension. Use your thumbs, elbows and even the heels of your feet to apply pressure here.

✳ Apply pressure all along both sides of the spine. Do this first with your palms then with your thumbs.

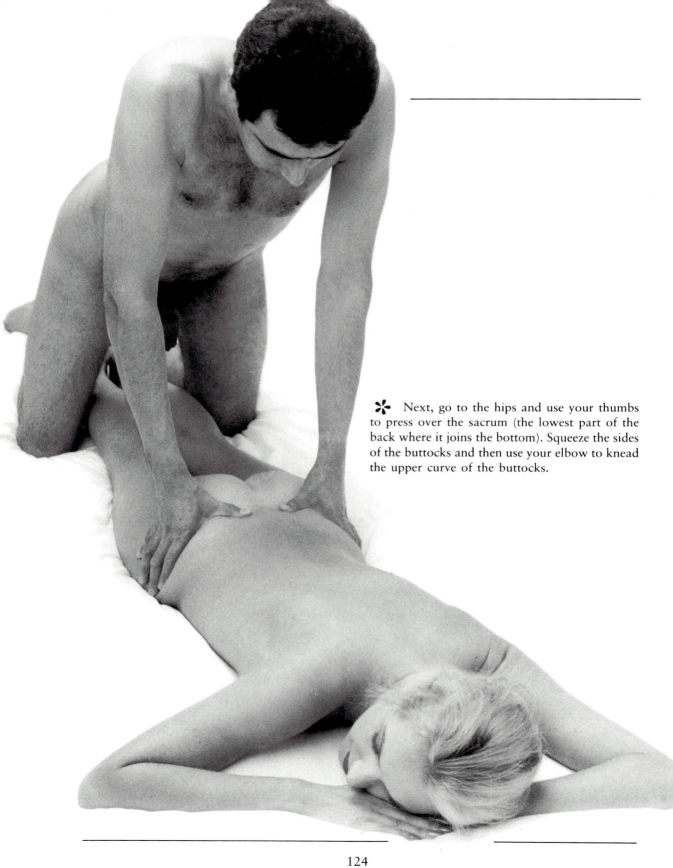

✳ Next, go to the hips and use your thumbs to press over the sacrum (the lowest part of the back where it joins the bottom). Squeeze the sides of the buttocks and then use your elbow to knead the upper curve of the buttocks.

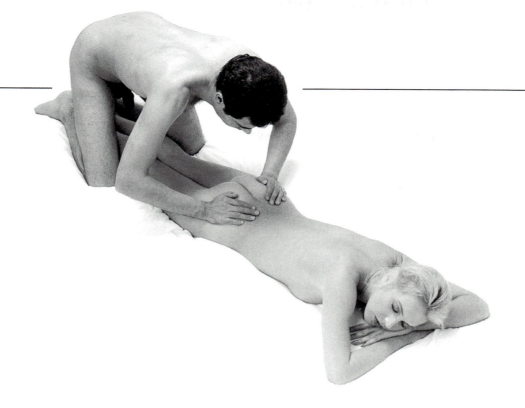

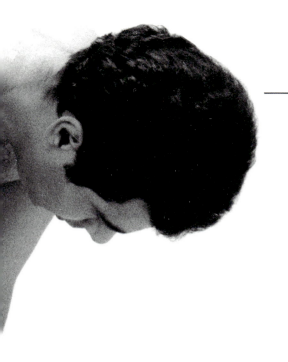

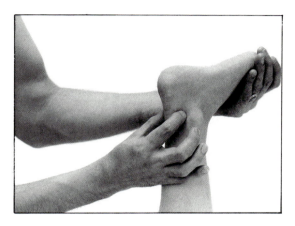

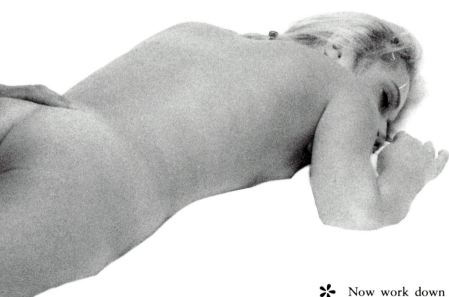

✳ Now work down the centre back of each leg, first with your palm and then your knees. Press lightly at the side of the Achilles tendon for about 3-5 seconds.

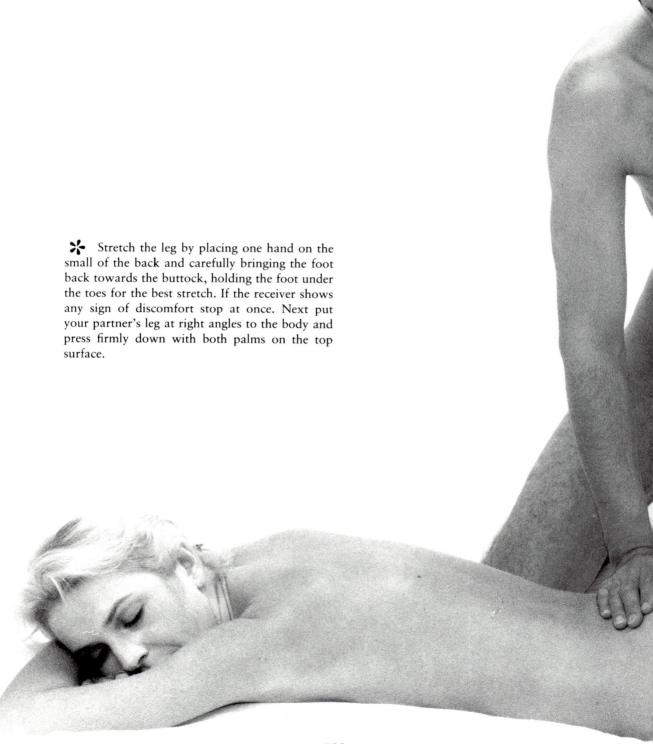

✳ Stretch the leg by placing one hand on the small of the back and carefully bringing the foot back towards the buttock, holding the foot under the toes for the best stretch. If the receiver shows any sign of discomfort stop at once. Next put your partner's leg at right angles to the body and press firmly down with both palms on the top surface.

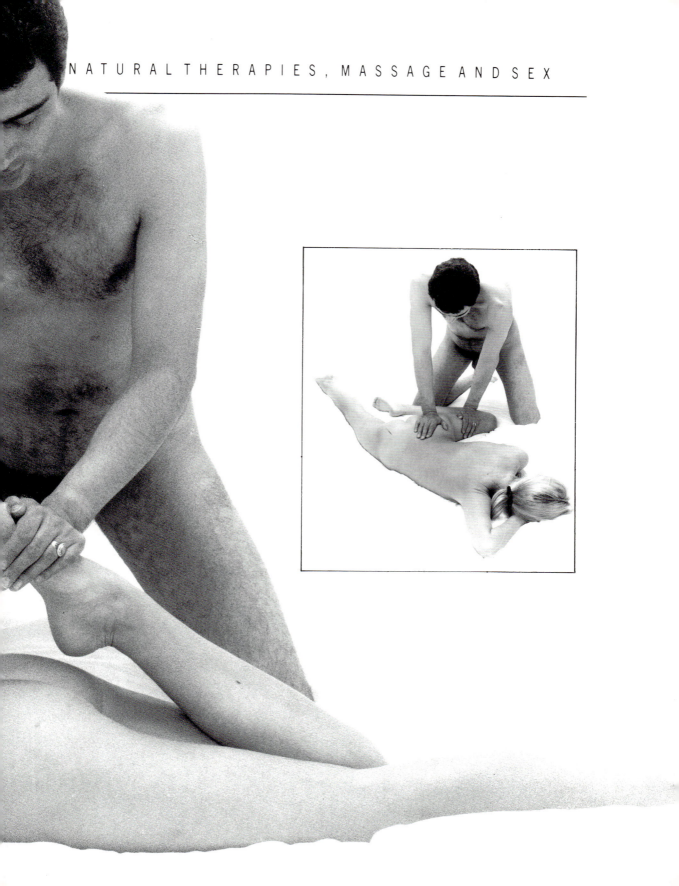

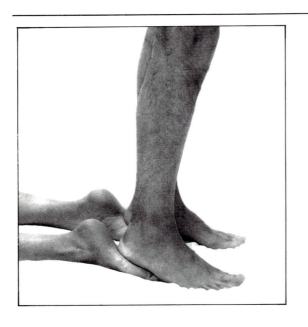

✳ Now walk on your partner's soles.

✳ Then massage the feet as outlined on page 52.

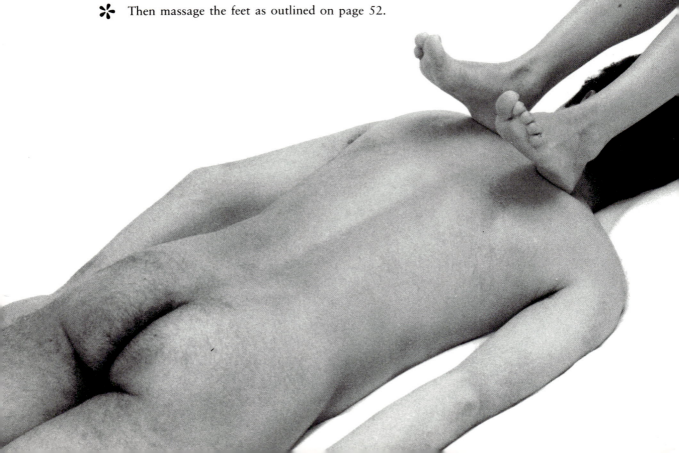

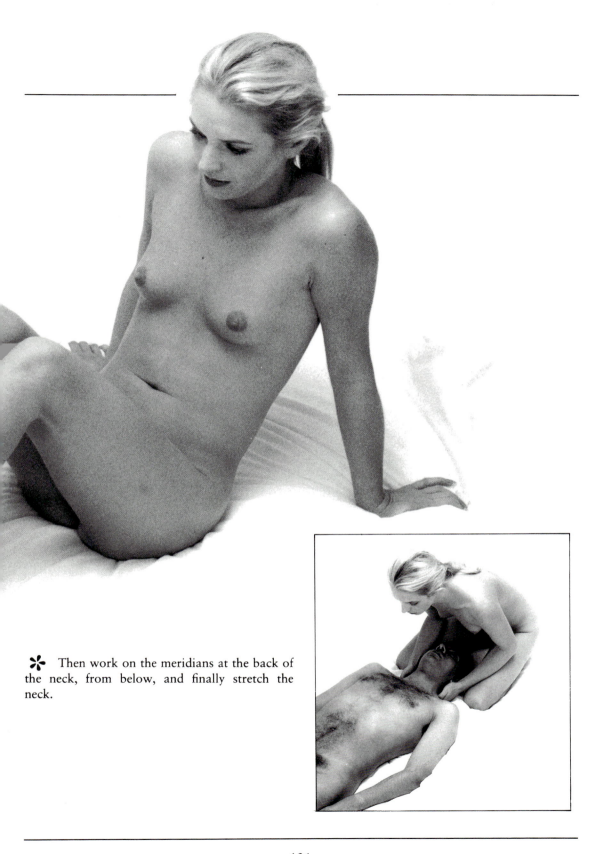

✳ Then work on the meridians at the back of the neck, from below, and finally stretch the neck.

✳ Work around the face as described on page 42.

✻ Turn next to the arms, applying palm pressure along each inner arm in turn with your partner's palm upwards.

✻ Apply palm pressure down the forearm, with his or her palm facing downwards.

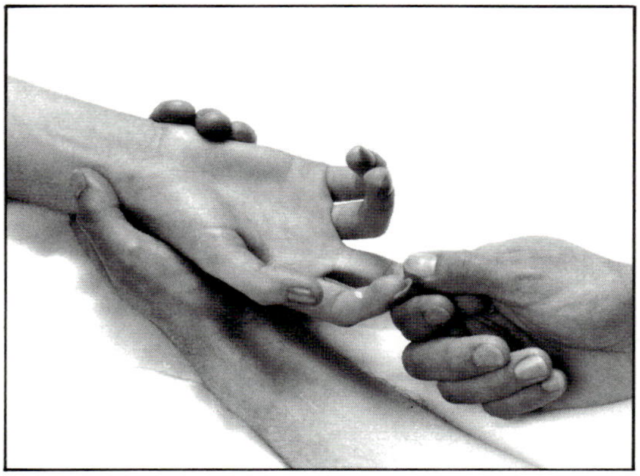

✲ Then turn your attention to the hands. Pull the fingers gently before going on to stimulate the area in the web between the thumb and the first finger. Press here for 5 seconds using your fingers on the palm side and your thumb on the top of his or her hand.

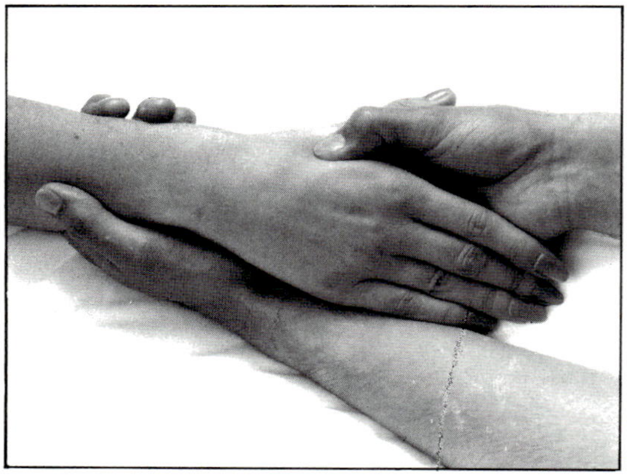

✲ Now take hold of your partner's hand at the wrist and gently shake the arm to loosen and relax it.

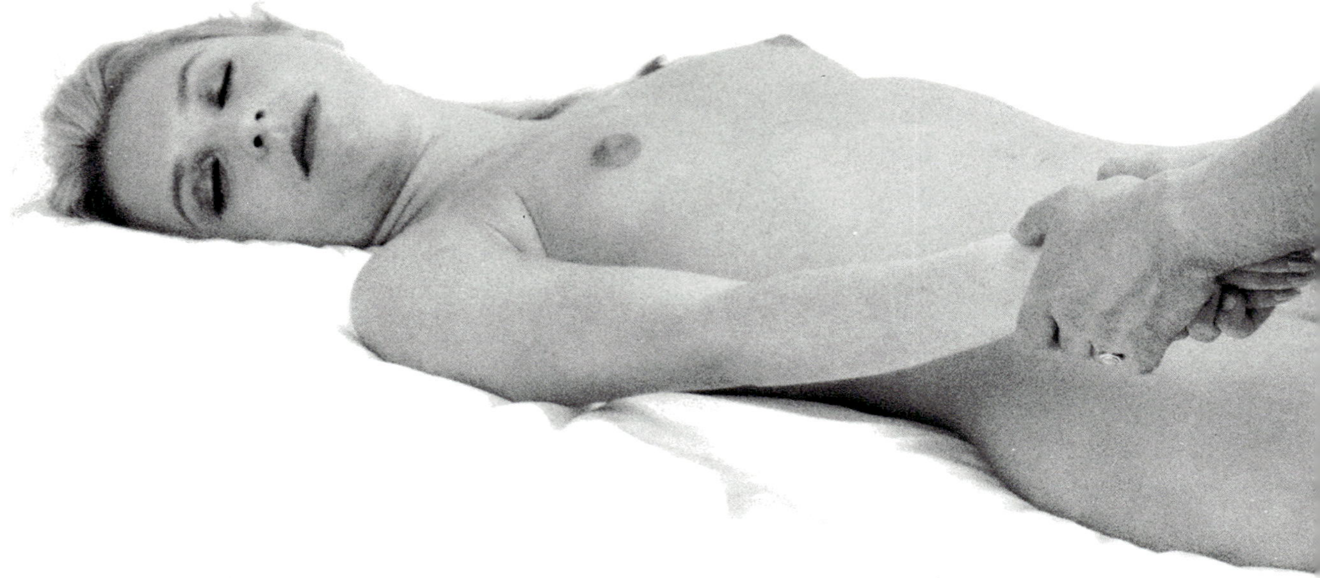

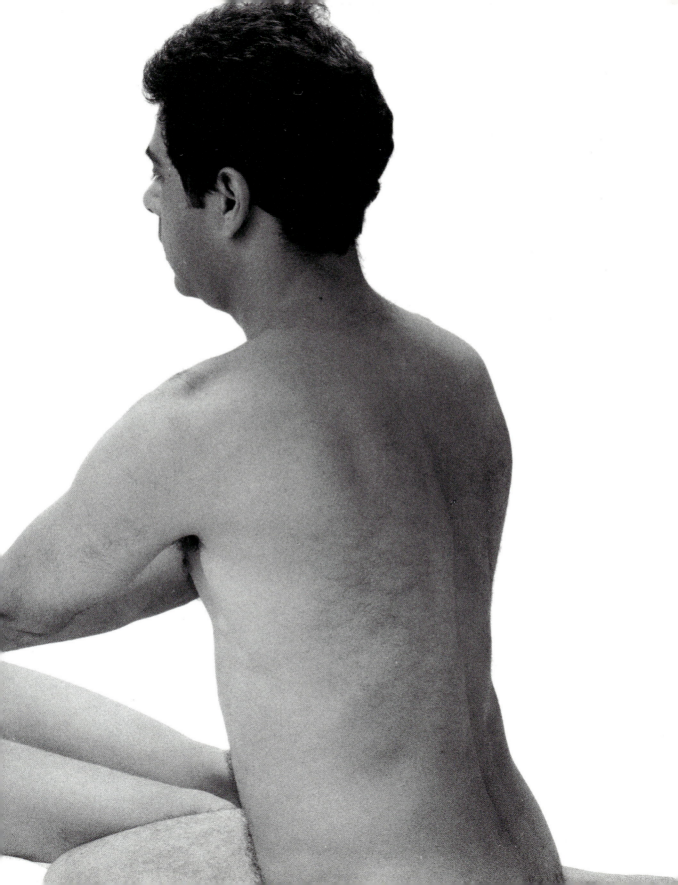

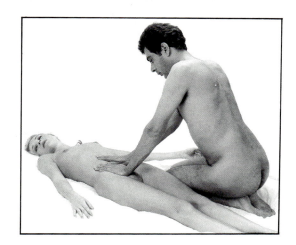

✳ Massage the lower area of the stomach – the *hara*. Work around the area clockwise, as outlined on page 49, then press gently under both sides of the ribs and down the midline to the navel.

✳ Complete your shiatsu massage by working down the fronts of the legs with palm pressure, first down the inside of the thigh and lower leg and then down the outside, avoiding pressure on the bone.

✳ Stretch the foot first backwards and then forwards and repeat the whole sequence on the other leg.

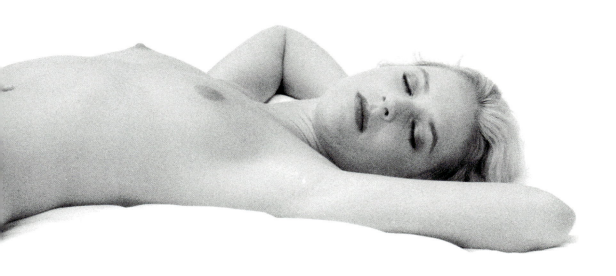

I must stress that this kind of shiatsu is a simple do-it-yourself, relaxing, pleasure-centred pursuit. It is *not* supposed to be directly 'healing' for any specific condition. It is safest to go to a professional therapist if you are searching for a cure of any kind.

Having said this, the rather different techniques involved here can be a pleasant change and can often have more profound mental and emotional effects than an ordinary sensual massage. In fact, some people find that, if it is done properly, a shiatsu massage can be very moving and can mobilise all kinds of emotions. It is vital therefore, that the person doing the giving can be trusted by the receiver. It is difficult or near impossible to relax completely and allow oneself to become totally vulnerable to one's feelings if one fears being let down, criticised, ridiculed, or ignored if emotions begin to surface.

As with all forms of massage, the main elements are understanding, love, trust and care, and the best massage experiences result from this empathy coming across to the receiver.

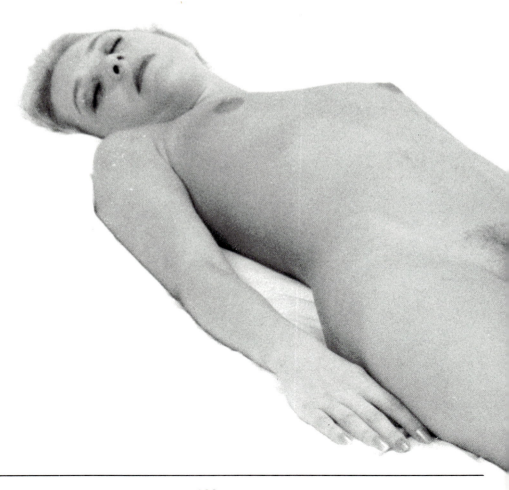

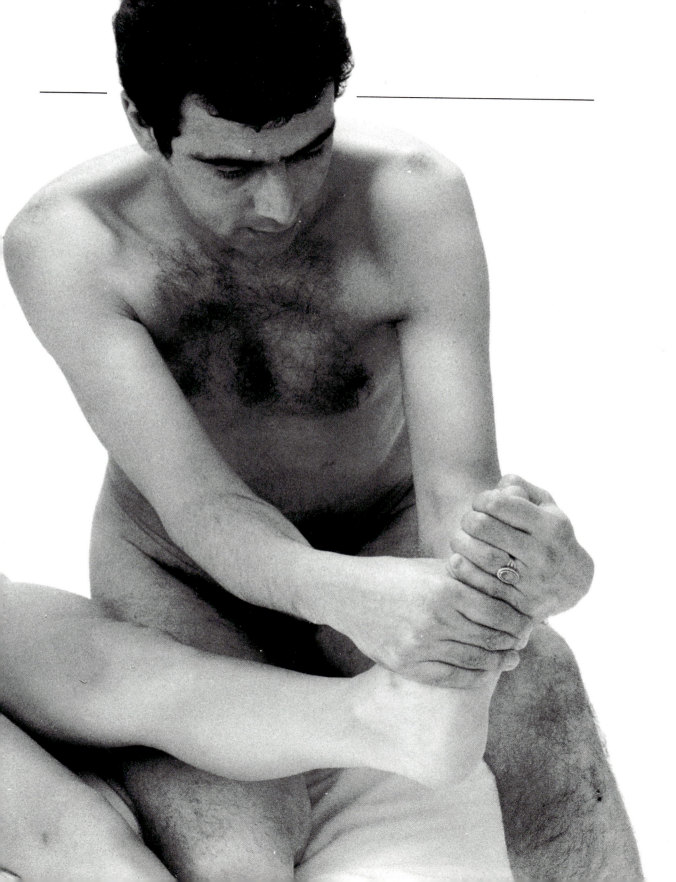

Acupressure

This is closely related to shiatsu, and there is little doubt that the correct stimulation of certain acupuncture points has a beneficial effect on the body, mind and spirit generally. Although no amateur massage enthusiast will ever become familiar enough with the acupuncture points to treat illnesses in any meaningful way, some of the points are easy to find and to apply pressure to, often with excellent results. This, then, is an add-on skill that can be used by any couple who already have sensual massage skills.

You simply use thumb pressure over the known acupuncture points to produce both local and distant effects on the body. Here are some suggestions. Press each point for about 4 seconds, two or three times.

BACK
● Each side of the spine.

● Along the shoulder ridge.

HIPS
● Sides of buttocks.

● Over sacrum.

● Centre of buttock crease.

ANKLES
● Both sides of Achilles tendon simultaneously.

FEET
● Centre of ball of foot.

● One or two inches above join between big toe and second toe.

SHOULDERS
● An inch or two below the hollow at the outer end of collarbone.

ARMS AND HANDS
● In the web between thumb and first finger.

HARA
● Three inches to either side of navel (press in towards navel).

● Press with flats of four fingers, two inches below navel, centrally.

LEGS
● Back of each knee.

● Top of shin bone, as in the illustration. Press hard. If you are on the correct point, a powerful sensation will run down to the ankle.

Pressure on these points often adds a special dimension to what would otherwise have been an ordinary, if pleasant, massage, and pressing over all of these areas is safe in healthy people, except for the area between the thumb and first finger, which should *not* be pressed in pregnant women.

If pressure anywhere causes pain or discomfort, however, stop at once and discuss the matter with an acupuncturist. You may simply have pressed too hard but it is always better not to make such assumptions.

Reflexology

Reflexology works on the basis that there are reflex zones in the soles of the feet corresponding to every part of the body. It is claimed that pressure and manipulation of these areas harmonise the energy flows in the body and make the receiver feel relaxed.

Learning reflexology is best done at a proper seminar or course and a book such as this is no place to go into any detail. Suffice it to say that massaging the feet can be very relaxing, if you follow certain basic tips.

The finger and thumb techniques of reflexology are rather different from normal massage and they really should be learned from an expert.

Do not attempt this kind of massage on pregnant women or anyone with severe varicose veins or phlebitis.

However, it is possible to massage the feet by using a simple reflexology technique. The best position for this is to have the receiver sitting in a reclining chair or in an ordinary, comfortable chair with his feet up on a stool, at the same level as your lap.

Oil is not the best lubricant for this kind of massage. Instead, try talcum powder or even cornflour. Place a towel on your lap and massage one foot at a time.

Now take one forefoot and, sandwiching it between your hands, move the front half of the foot backwards and forwards. Then support the heel of the foot in one hand while you rotate the front of the foot with the other.

To work on the whole foot, grasp the toes with your thumb on the big toe and your other fingers holding the receiver's other toes. This fixes the foot and slightly stretches the sole. Now take the thumb of the hand you intend to use and bend it at the first joint to barely a right angle. Place the tip of this bent thumb on the sole of the receiver's foot and, working the bent joint, 'walk' your thumb along the foot. The receiver should not feel your nail if you have your thumb in the correct position. For the best possible results, the inside edge of your thumb should be the area that is in contact with the various zones of the foot (not the actual tip). Because the reflex points are located under the skin quite deep pressure is needed to affect them.

It is not wise to massage the feet in this way if someone is unwell. However, for a relaxing and toning treatment you can start at the toes and slowly work your way down to the heels after studying the layout of the main reflex zones in the diagram. When you have completed massaging the sole, begin work on the sides of the feet.

As you walk your thumb over the skin, be careful if you come to any areas of tenderness or grittiness because if you press too hard here the individual will be tensed rather than relaxed.

End by holding the foot and rotating it, as you did when you started, then briefly hold the foot between both of your hands. Repeat the whole process on the other foot.

If you have done this well, your partner or friend will be very relaxed. This is a very pleasant

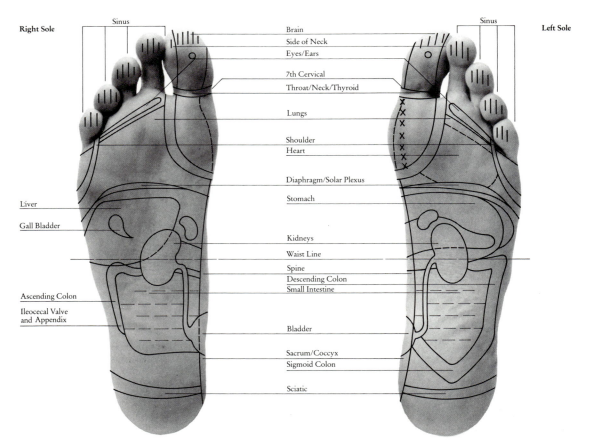

Right Sole — Left Sole

Sinus — Sinus
Brain
Side of Neck
Eyes/Ears
7th Cervical
Throat/Neck/Thyroid
Lungs
Shoulder
Heart
Diaphragm/Solar Plexus
Stomach
Liver
Gall Bladder
Kidneys
Waist Line
Spine
Descending Colon
Small Intestine
Ascending Colon
Ileocecal Valve and Appendix
Bladder
Sacrum/Coccyx
Sigmoid Colon
Sciatic

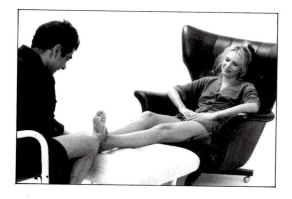

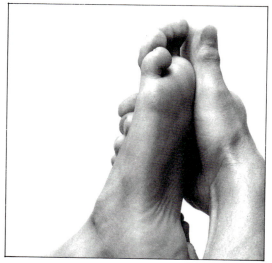

way to relax a friend whom you do not know sufficiently well to do a whole body massage on.

Some people enjoy receiving a hand massage performed in much the same way. This, too, works on the principle that parts of the body are represented in the reflex zones of the hands.

In conclusion

Although none of the 'alternative' massage methods I have briefly outlined in this section are erotic in themselves, many couples find them either stimulating or relaxing and this can be the starting point for an erotic massage. An individual whose feet have just been massaged using reflexology techniques or someone who has had their acupuncture points massaged systematically might well feel so relaxed that they want to have sex, perhaps after some erotic massage.

But as I have stressed through the book all of these methods—apart, of course, from erotic massage itself—should be seen simply as 'gifts' from the giver to the receiver. Unless a couple agree beforehand that sex is to be the end-point, it is far better to leave things to take their course and see what happens as the session progresses. Some people start off just asking for their feet to be massaged, for example, and begin to feel not only extremely relaxed but even sexually aroused.

It is important to remember that, whatever we do with our partner, it should be the joy of giving that lies at the heart of any good massage. But this needs to be matched by the receiver being at one with the giver, in tune with his or her efforts so that the massage time is rewarding for both. This leads to communication, both verbal and non-verbal, at the time of the massage, or afterwards. Such two-way communication is central to all massage, of whatever kind, and it is this that makes massage so magical a pursuit for many couples.

In an age of goal-centred sex and worries about sexual performance this giving and receiving of one another freely is arguably one of the most priceless gifts in a loving relationship.

INDEX